T0156945

OLD SCHOOL SELLING:

The truth about Sales, selling, getting the right job, and the skills you need to be a #1 Salesperson in the 21st Century

The real scoop on what it takes to make it in Sales and be number one, and how to get the right job at the right company the first time around, as told by a Master Salesman with 42 years of experience and tens of millions of dollars in results...

JOSEPH SOKOLOFF &

DOUGLAS SOKOLOFF

iUniverse, Inc.
New York   Bloomington

iUniverse books may be ordered through booksellers or by contacting:

iUniverse
1663 Liberty Drive
Bloomington, IN 47403
www.iuniverse.com
1-800-Authors (1-800-288-4677)

Because of the dynamic nature of the Internet, any Web
addresses or links contained in this book may have changed
since publication and may no longer be valid. The views
expressed in this work are solely those of the author and do
not necessarily reflect the views of the publisher, and the
publisher hereby disclaims any responsibility for them.

ISBN: 978-1-4502-3475-7 (sc)

Printed in the United States of America

iUniverse rev. date: 9/23/2010

INTRODUCTION

My name is Joe Sokoloff, and I recently ended a forty two year career in commission Sales. Every day of those forty two years was spent either as a Sales person, a Sales Manager, or as President, supervising commissioned Sales people (while still selling myself).

Later in my career, even as the president of a company, I was on a salary plus commission. Perhaps unusual, but that's the way I wanted it. Why would I want to be on commission after so many years, and after having made it to the top? Because early on in my career after selling successfully for a few years I realized it was the only way I could maintain some control over my life. If you're the number one Sales person in an organization you can tell the president to screw off (perhaps in a nicer way) and believe it or not, you can get away with it most of the time. But trust me, don't try it unless you're VERY secure in your position.

In this book I am going to tell you what I think about commission Sales, and what I learned during the last 42 years. More importantly, I am going to tell you what I see as the pluses and minuses in 2010 and beyond for anyone contemplating a career in commission Sales.

For those considering a career in Sales, the first thing you should ask yourself is; why do I want to be in Sales? It's the question that almost nobody I have ever met in Sales has asked themselves before coming into it, including myself. If they did have a reason, it was usually the wrong one, such as, "I like people", "I want to contribute to a company", or, "my father is in Sales", which for the record, are ALL terrible answers. The only right answer is, "I want to make a ton of money!!!".

Just in case you are wondering what makes me qualified to tell you how to sell, on the last page of the book you will find copies of my W2's from the last 3 years before I retired in 2007.

MY STORY

It was 1964 and I had a young wife who had just dropped a new child in my lap less than 24 months after we had been married, not to mention that we were living in a one bedroom apartment and money was tight. Sound familiar?

When I was first married in 1962 I was earning $100.00 dollars a week – that's $5,000 a year - as a travel agent (all salary) and my wife was earning $75.00 a week as a clerical worker for a large publishing company. This presented a problem after our first child was born, as her $75.00 a week disappeared when she could no longer work, which meant I was now in deep trouble. Keep in mind that this was 1962, and even then $100 bucks didn't go very far, so losing $75 a week (40% of all of our income) was devastating.

I thought about my quandary for a day or two, and once I was over the shock of my circumstances I said to myself, what have you accomplished so far? I had a B.S. (no pun intended) degree in Business Administration, but what was I really qualified to do? What had I really learned about business, or anything in the real world for that matter? The answer; NOTHING! That degree was as useful as tits on a bull! Even worse yet, my degree came from a third rate University – basically a waste of four years of time and a lot of money. Business Administration, even today, does little to prepare you for a career in Sales, though perhaps it might be helpful if you wanted to be an Economist, but I don't know too many Economists.

My education had basically prepared me to go from college into my fathers business, which I could have easily done without having wasted four years and thousands of dollars, not to mention that within a year of my leaving college my fathers business was no longer in existence, so this left me on the street to fend for myself. After a couple of meaningless jobs I became a Travel Agent, a career that was safe and fun, but not terribly lucrative.

Why do I tell you this sad tale of woe? To point out that I was just like many of you, and that you are not alone if you have ever been put in, or you are now in a corner.

I was on the spot with no marketable skills and no prospects. In my mind I had only one option to make any real money and control my destiny; become a Salesman. The reality is, that's how many people got into Sales back then, as a last resort, and for that matter, the way that many people still do today.

No one ever said to me when I was in college in the 1950's, or in fact at any time afterward, "Joe, sit down and review your skills, here is a checklist to fill out; evaluate your attributes - the pluses and minuses". I never met with a career counselor in High School or College, nor was it ever suggested. Perhaps you have been luckier than I was and you have had that advantage. I did the only thing I could, I registered with the school business referral service (an early version of Campus Recruiting and Job

Placement), but I never received a single call for an interview. I was a "B" student with slightly above middle of the class ranking. I also had another disadvantage, I was a Jew, and to add insult to injury, I had an easily identifiable ethnic last name. In the 1950's, most major U S companies didn't hire Jews. Times have changed since then, but the fact is, there are still plenty of prejudiced people who have hiring authority, so the reality is that race, creed, and ethnicity can still unknowingly be an issue. However, the great thing about Sales today is that a successful Salesperson could be from Mars or Pluto, and any smart company or hiring manager will likely look beyond any underlying prejudice they may have in order to get that person working for them and do their best to make them happy. The moral to the story is; Sales (and money) trumps everything, even prejudice.

So, back to my story; I was in a bad situation that was rapidly getting worse, one that hopefully none of you reading this will ever end up in – it was dire. But, that is the best thing about Sales, ANYONE CAN DO IT! But you have to really want it!

Things have changed in many ways since the 1950's and 1960's, most importantly, communications; Fax Machines, Voicemail, Caller ID, Cell Phones, and perhaps most significantly, the internet and email, which have opened up a huge channel of easy to identify job opportunities. Universities also do a better job of preparing their students for the business world, as well as helping with career counseling in many cases, though there is still no accredited degree program or an advanced degree track for people wishing to pursue a career in Sales, and very few Colleges even offer courses focusing on Sales in the real world.

In my opinion selling is a career, and very few Universities give it the respect that it deserves, and in doing so they are failing to meet a tremendous need.

According to the *United States Bureau of Labor and Statistics*, as of 2006, there were 8,600,000 people working in Sales in either Manufacturers and Wholesale Sales, Real Estate, Construction, Technical and scientific products, Insurance, and Financial Services. This obviously doesn't include all of the Sales jobs out there, but it should give you a pretty good idea that Sales makes up a big part of our economy and a big percentage of all of the jobs out there.

I became a successful salesman my first time out, starting from scratch - with zero skills – which was also a straight commission job (no base salary). When I took this job my back was against the wall with no fallback plan or cushion; it was sink or swim, literally. My family was depending on me and there was no room for error, no acceptable outcome except success. My advice to you is, don't allow yourself to get in the same predicament. Plan ahead and think ahead!

First and foremost, to be successful in Sales means setting a personal goal of being NUMBER ONE! This requires two key factors; motivation and desire. For some people these two overlap.

I can sum up the rest of this book for you right now; this is about the facts of life in Sales. These are the facts, like it or not, whether you plan to make a career out of Sales, or even if you don't and it is simply a temporary way to make a living. This book is the result of what only 42 years in any career can give you; Experience. My hope is that when you are done reading this that some of it will sink in and you will walk away with some better direction, knowledge, and most important of all, confidence. I have already done it, so this isn't preaching, it is teaching, and your learning, believing, and succeeding out in the real world will be MY payoff!

CHAPTER ONE:
GETTING STARTED

Lets start with a check list of what I believe are the necessary ingredients to make a successful Salesperson. You decide how to tailor this to fit your your own life with the premise being, if you choose Sales as a career, why be anything less than the very best?

What should "being the very best" mean to you? One thing, and one thing only; **MONEY**! Your priority every day should be money first, money second, and money third. If you do not buy that idea, you should immediately do two things; first, don't read any further, you will be wasting your time, and second, don't go into Sales! If money isn't first second and third on your list of career priorities, then Sales is not for you.

Sound too tough? Cold Hearted? Pessimistic? Well, life is tough, get used to it!

Once I finally grew up and really matured, which for me was at the age of 32, I decided I did not ever again want be second best at anything I did. I related my career and my success to money and nothing else, and you should do the same. Believe me when I tell you, saying you want to be number one is a lot easier than actually doing it.

Have you ever heard the expression, "GREAT SALES PEOPLE ARE BORN". Now that is total bullshit (pardon my French…..)! Most naturally talented Sales people fail. The reason is that they have too much talent and confidence, and not enough of the other skills needed to survive in the real world, such as discipline, follow through, organization, and patience. And take it from me, I am the greatest example of an un-naturally talented Sales person, but I learned and developed all of the other key skills and attributes. The key words in that sentence are "learned" and "developed". Remember that…

So let's get into that checklist. The list is in the order of their relative importance. Can you succeed without them all? Of course you can, but can you be number one in your Sales organization without them? In my opinion, and based on my experience, it is highly improbable and highly unlikely.

THE INGREDIANTS CHECK LIST:

1. **DESIRE**
2. **MOTIVATION**
3. **MATURITY**
4. **FOLLOW THROUGH**
5. **DISCIPLINE**
6. **COMMON SENSE**
7. **BASIC WRITING AND GRAMMAR SKILLS**
8. **NEAT AND CLEAN APPEARANCE**
9. **PROFESSIONALISM**
10. **AVERAGE INTELLIGENCE OR BETTER**

Seems easy enough, right? Well, take an honest look in the mirror; do you have all of the items on the list? If not, perhaps it's time to make some changes, or explore other career options. Note discipline is interchangeable with maturity.

CHAPTER TWO:
DESIRE

We all know what its like to want something badly; The Red Porsche with the 400hp engine, a trip to Hawaii, those expensive designer shoes, a new 60" Flat Screen TV. I could go on and on, but that's not the point of this. What I am talking about is the one out of every hundred Sales people that I have met in the last 42 years who wanted to be in Sales for the "Right Reasons". The majority of the Sales people I have encountered over the years did not have "it", which means they simply didn't have the desire. Just being a Sales person, doesn't automatically give you desire or drive, nor does the designation alone make you a "great" Sales Person. The same could be said for Doctors and Lawyers, however, in many Professional careers, educational requirements and professional licensing ensures a minimum level of education, skill, and commitment. Most people in sales think they are great (ironically as do most doctors and lawyers), or the best, but then again, everyone thinks they are good looking and funny, and obviously everyone isn't. A career in Sales doesn't have any of that, which is a positive because it means that anyone can do it, but it is also a negative, again, because anyone can do it...

MEASURE YOU OWN DESIRE FOR A CAREER IN SALES. DO YOU WANT TO LIVE THIS KIND OF LIFE?

1. Control of your day and your time

2. Plan your schedule (in detail) weeks in advance

3. Organize your next days work the night before

4. No boss over your shoulder. You will be your own best friend, since most commissioned Sales people are alone 90+% of the time.

Is this you? In simple terms, can you manage and handle this kind of lifestyle? Rain, snow, or hail, you need to be out there making contact with people who in most cases don't really care if they see you, and in more than a few cases don't want to see you.

I've said it a thousand times; you could stand on the corner of 42nd Street & 5th Avenue during the middle of a business day in Manhattan and try giving away gold bricks, and few people would even stop to look and see if you really had a real gold brick in your hand. Even a megaphone wouldn't help. So, since you aren't likely trying to give away gold bricks, you are at an even greater disadvantage and you need real desire to overcome the lack of interest that is going to be shown to you day in and day out. Rejection is everywhere in Sales, and one of the few things that is guaranteed.

Liking people, being outgoing, and finding it easy to talk to people is not a good reason to go into Sales; Sales is not a social arena. Personally I was never that outgoing as a child or even as an adult. In fact I was a rather withdrawn child, and I was the kid who was picked last whenever we had pick up games.

So, what was my motivation to get into Sales? As I said in the introduction, I was corned like a rat without any skills; I fell into Sales as a last resort. This is not a good reason for you or anyone to go into Sales either, I just got lucky. Ideally and preferably, you should seriously consider your options and evaluate the factors involved in this career, which is exactly what we will do in this book. We will look at the pluses and minuses which I outline, and you will make a lifestyle choice, which is a much better way to choose a Sales career, and "choose" is the key word. Don't do what I did – it wasn't a choice; a choice infers that you have options, and I had none.

Desire, if I can sum it up simply, is looking at the facts and the challenges in front of you, as well as the potential rewards, and saying to yourself, this is what I want, and I can do it. Ideally, whatever it is that you are looking at is a perfect fit, but as we all know, perfect fits in life are rare, so perhaps it only fits you 75 or 80% . You will have to be the judge of what is an acceptable fit.

Chapter Three:
Motivation...Do You Have It?

Nobody else can give you motivation; you have to find it within yourself. So, the question is, why be a Sales person?

What are the two biggest pluses to being a Sales person?

- You can control your income if you are a commissioned or partially commissioned
- You can work at your own pace and set your own schedule

The funny thing is, the two biggest pluses are also the two biggest potential minuses, but of course, whether or not they will be minuses, will depend on you.

Many Sales people work out of company offices that have a structured Sales organization, including things such as regularly scheduled Sales meetings, reporting of Sales calls, meetings, training, manager shadowing, and often set office hours. A pretty basic rule of thumb is that the more commission oriented the job, the less structured the Sales organization, and the less time you spend in the office. In the mostly or straight commission scenario, what you do with your time, and what you make of it, is solely up to you. Why? Because the company has nothing to lose, only you do. Commission only Sales is not a team sport! You can work fast, slow, backwards, forwards, it's up to you. You are the boss of your own time and the sole factor in what your income will be.

Any time that I was ever required to attend a one or two day Sales meeting, I always spent the breaks in a phone booth (in the days before cell phones and laptops) booking appointments and doing follow ups. In the two or three breaks a day I had during one of these long meetings or training sessions, I picked up 5 or 6 appointments. Sound crazy or too extreme? Maybe you don't want it bad enough? While the other guys were out having lunch or drinks, I was on the phone dialing for dollars. I was never one of the "guys", but then again, I never cared. Those "guys", didn't all have a mortgage and a wife and two kids to feed, or perhaps if they did, they didn't care as much as I did, and in turn the net result was that not one of them ever made as much money as I did.

The company or sales manager you work for should not be your primary motivation. You should be! Sales contests and the posting of Sales people's results are definitely helpful, as they appeal to peoples vanity, self esteem and ego, however, if that's what it takes to get you going, in the long run you will not be a success, let alone number one.

Motivation is best set by you and comes from within. Making the most money possible should be your primary motivation, and as far as I am concerned it should be 95% of it. Self esteem, ego, and vanity are ok for the other 5%, but not for much more.

Many years ago I read an AMA (American Marketing Association) national survey of Sales people that ranked money fourth on the list of reasons people were in Sales. I would venture to guess that in the years since that it may have moved up a notch to number 3, but not much more, as the economy and technology may have changed radically since then, but people as a rule don't change that much. This points out a simple fact; most people in Sales do not belong in this profession. Note that I called it a "profession", because to the winners that's what it is, a profession and a career.

In Sales, money is both the arbiter and barometer for success – effectively the judge and jury - as it is the only direct correlation between effort and result, and the only barometer for success. Making one thousand Sales calls with one closed sale does not make you a success; however, making one hundred Sales calls with twenty closed Sales does. If you do not agree, it's simple; don't become a Sales person. This isn't a subjective opinion, it is a fact, and it is motivation in its truest form. Everything else is pure bullshit!

Be honest with yourself, and ask yourself this question; do you have the Motivation? If the answer is yes, read on......

CHAPTER FOUR:
MATURITY.....

Most people in their twenties have absolutely no idea who they are yet, what they are capable of, or what they want to do with their lives. A professor at a University recently told me about a survey that said most 20 year olds today will go through five career changes between now and retirement. Read that again, not JOB changes, CAREER changes!

Most people spend 33% (40 hours) of their available time during the full 120 hours available to them from Monday through Friday, working. Many people spend upwards of 40% of that time, or 10 hours a day working; therefore wouldn't you assume it is worth putting a lot of time and thought into the decisions about your career? Have you? The reality is, that's not how it works with most individuals. Most of the people I have come in contact with over the years have not ended up in the career that was their first choice, or even their second or third choice, and in many cases, it wasn't a choice at all. You make a choice to become a Doctor, Lawyer, Teacher, or Police Officer, because it requires specific schooling, training, and licensing, but for many people" jobs" aren't choices, and they are most certainly not careers.

Obviously you are making a clear choice and decision by going into the aforementioned "careers", but what about Sales? Do you know a university that offers a four year education in Sales, or even Sales Management? How about Sales Administration? Very few Business Schools offer any course work at all in practical Sales, and even those few programs that are available do not focus on real world practical Sales at any level of depth other than from a one dimensional text book approach, which frankly isn't going to help you very much. Furthermore, do you think the professors are seasoned, experienced, and more importantly successful former or current number one Sales people? The answer is, of course not, they are Academics, not successful Salespeople.

Most people in their twenties do not have the maturity or discipline to go about selecting a career. Did your parents sit you down in high school and have an in depth discussion with you about your future and your career? Did they then follow up with you on a regular basis to help you come to some conclusions on your future education and career goals? I can tell you that my parent did not, but that was a different time, and my parents were immigrants from Europe whose first language was not English, however, even today, I doubt it happens very often, even in the best American Upper Middle Class homes. If it did happen to you, consider yourself one of the lucky few, but realize that you are in the small minority.

Being in Sales requires a maturity far beyond that of the average individual in their early twenties. The fact is, most people I have encountered in my career didn't have that kind of maturity until they were over thirty. As I said earlier, maturity goes hand and hand with motivation, so it's simple, without maturity its very hard to have motivation.

CHAPTER FIVE:
FINDING THE RIGHT OPPORTUNITY…
THE FIRST TIME

Finding the right job or opportunity is the key to your success, but how exactly do you find the right one the FIRST time?

Many Sales jobs in today's market are either dead end or of questionable integrity (read: scams). Sound like a black hole? Not at all, as there are still plenty of good high earning potential Sales positions in the market place regardless of whether the economy is up or down. Every company will always need to sell their products or services, regardless of the state of the economy. You just have to investigate carefully and filter out the good ones.

In a bad economy, companies may be cutting back in a lot of areas, but Sales is usually the opposite, as when the economy is bad companies need good Sales people even more, and they usually ramp up their Sales efforts when the economy is bad. That being said, you will need to search hard, exercise caution, do your homework, and check out prospective opportunities like your life depended on it, as in fact, it does. This is your livelihood and your life we are talking about! Would you choose a doctor to treat you for a serious illness without doing research on him? Of course not! So, why would you take a gamble on your livelihood with a company you don't know anything about? Do your homework first.

Remember, a salary position in Sales generally equals a dead end – it has no potential. The more commission versus the salary, the greater the potential to make a really good income. This of course assumes that you want to be number one in the company you are working for, and therefore you are willing to fulfill all the responsibilities outlined in this book. Remember, most commission jobs offer a "draw" that pays you while you're getting off the ground. A "Draw", is a salary that is drawn against future commission earnings, so technically the company is advancing you money against money you have not yet earned, but that you will hopefully earn in the future. Any money/commission you make over your draw each year is pure commission owed to you. Many companies, assuming you perform well, will wipe out any deficits owed in your draw during your first 6 months or year of employment. This is an important question to ask during your second interview, but we will get into that later in the book.

Company cars and expense allowances all figure into a total compensation package along with your salary and/or commission. These benefits are a percentage of Sales that is calculated by the company as the cost of selling. So here is the best part; management bases all these costs on what the average Sales person will earn, not what the top Sales people earn. Remember, 80% of the Sales at most companies come from the top 20% of the Sales force.

In my first Sales job, the average Sales person in my division produced two to three Sales a week. Now there were 250 Sales people, so if you had five Sales a week in that Sales force, you were near the top and you were golden. Stupid inexperienced and naive me; I didn't know that I was supposed to be average. I had a wife, a kid, a lousy used car and a crummy one bedroom apartment. I was given a territory that over the previous 20 years had been a total failure, and consistently one of the lowest performing. In fact, most of the time over those 20 years it had no Sales person even covering it. Obviously I was never told any of this by the company or by my manager at the time, but by and by I learned this information after I was with the company for about a year.

There were seven other Sales territories working out of my office, and on average a Sales territory turned over a Sales person every 4 - 5 months. Some of the Sales people did little if any Sales at all. God knows why they stayed or why the company kept them, but this was the way things were done back then.

My Sales manager was 500 miles away from my territory and I saw him every three to four weeks, but in the first four months he came out and worked with me at least one or two times a month to make Sales calls with me. I memorized almost everything he said because I did not understand anything about the product or how it worked.

I had desire, motivation, and with dumb luck, I had a good opportunity. My first year I wrote an average of 4 orders each week. After 8 months of excellent production the president was curious if I was an anomaly, lucky, or putting in fake orders. Unlike most new Sales people, I was succeeding, so he sent a regional manager from the South who didn't know me to spend a day with me. The Regional Manager went back to the home office and told the President of the company, "Check all his orders, he has no idea what the hell he is doing!" The fact was, he was partially right, I had no clue what I was doing, but he was wrong about one important thing, all of my orders were valid, every single one of them. I had ignored the fact that I had no idea what I was doing, and that I had no idea about our product beyond the basics, but I didn't think about that, I thought about my wife and my kids, and ran for my life, like each dollar I had made might be my last. The idea of having to face my family and tell them we had no money for the things we needed was not something I could even fathom so I just kept on running and never stopped to look back.

Following this episode, the company decided to run a training class at the home office on product knowledge. What was the result? After the training I closed even more Sales, though I am not quite sure how, as the company ran a half-ass one week training program. However, after the training I was now bringing in 9 to 10 orders a week, which was unheard of in any territory prior to this class. The final result, I quickly became the number one Sales person nationally out of 250. I was now earning three times my starting income and things were going great. In my third year I was closing almost 50% of my presentations, an unheard of statistic in any product area involving Sales.

Naturally, bad news is always right around the corner. Because of my success, the company President wanted me to become the Sales Manager in New York City. I would soon find out that what should have been the top district in the country, had over time become a complete disaster. Here's how management put it to me, "take the job or we will cut your current territory by 2/3. After much thought and a lot of convincing by my wife, Sales Manager, and my father in law, I accepted the job.

The ironic thing about Sales is that a great Sales Person makes far more money than a great Sales Manager, so a promotion isn't correlated with a raise in income, so my income actually went down. Would I have done the same thing today? No way, I would have quit on the spot and immediately gotten a better paying job with my successful track record. But that was the sixties, so as I will point out by example several times in this book, "Do as I say, not as I did".

Experience is a great teacher, but unfortunately you don't get "do-over's" in life. On my first day in New York in my new job, I discovered that it was even far worse than I had been told, which I explain later on in the book.

A final thought to remember on the subject of management; "Great players don't always make great coaches, and great coaches were often never great players".

CHAPTER SIX:

ORGANIZATION...

Assuming you have done everything else right up to this point, we are now at one of the toughest parts. Why? Because it's a grind.

Organization is one of the keys to success in Sales, as well as most careers. It is a day in and day out responsibility. You can't fake organization. If you're smart enough and mature enough to select a great position, recognize that you can't get to your goal of being at the top without great effort, and it starts with organization. It's make or break.

I did well in my first two Sales jobs, and between them I spent fifteen years at those two companies, something fairly uncommon, if not unheard of today. In my first job, I sat down once a month, usually on a Sunday, laid out my account cards on the living room floor and selected by geographic location where I planned to be for the next 20 working days. Each day I then further broke down the calls by the order of location using a map, a task that was far more time consuming in the pre-internet days, and what is today a simple task. The time spent doing this assured the least amount of travel between calls, and guaranteed the most effective use of my time. I gained back ten fold the time spent organizing in the time saved and results I achieved.

Every Monday I went to the office with my planned calls for the week, got on the phone and attempted to book my appointments. Back in the 1960's it was a lot easier than today to get appointments. The pace of business has picked up dramatically; as has the volume of solicitations the average decision maker or manager at a large company receives. That combined with voicemail and caller ID has made using the phone as a primary tool for selling today a far more difficult and uncommon task. Cold calls, or canvassing, was also a primary and effective source of getting meetings back then, but it has no longer been a viable possibility since the 90's, and most notably September 11th, as even small companies in small cities have strict security policies, and no appointment means no entry, even into the building. Today, the phone along with email is a better combination. Back then, each Monday I usually took 75 to 100 account cards, got on the phone at 8am and worked non stop till 5pm, with no lunch. On a good day I was usually able to secure 25 appointments. Sound like a lot? It was my company's policy that you went door to door carrying a sample product that weighted 10 pounds with you. Start at the top of an office building and go office to office and canvas. I did that for two months, and it happened to be in July and August. I decided that I would die from heat stroke if I kept doing it their way, so I came up with my own idea; use the telephone. I was calling on Presidents and Treasurers of large and small companies, as well as law firms and accounting firms, and my system worked!

All companies have organizational systems that they introduce to their Sales force, some good, and some not so good. Some insist they be followed to the letter, others, usually smaller and more entrepreneurial firms have some flexibility. Remember, it's your life and your career. If you come up with what you think will work after properly testing it, and it's a better way to sell your product or service, then do it! Most companies aren't as concerned with methods or process as they are about results, and in the event they are, if after careful consideration you still think your way is more effective (read: you and the company will both make more money), as the old expression goes, "sometimes it is easier to ask for forgiveness than it is to ask for permission".

The President of my company at the time hated my working by appointment, he was from the old school (which today is the old, old, old school!) and had 25 years with the company. The funny thing was, he stopped complaining (to me at least) and did nothing to stop me once he saw the results. Later, when I became the District Sales Manager I taught all of my Sales people the same system. The results of implementing my system were astounding; my district became the number one district in the country for three years running. A few years later when I became Regional Sales Manager in charge of 8 districts, the same result came for all of the districts in my region. The lesson here; if it works and gets results -- and results mean only one thing, closed Sales - no one will stand in your way.

The funny thing was, the President still hated me because I didn't do it his way. So knowing I reached my ceiling at this company, after 10 years, I left the company. Both they and I knew one thing for sure; it was their loss.

****

Back to Organization; what is it really? It is simply the maturity to set a plan in place and follow it, without fail, day in and day out, week in and week out, year in and year out. This is by no means an easy task. This means recording and monitoring your results after every call, which today is made far easier by using one of the many Contact Management software programs available. Many companies have their own programs they require their Sales people to use that are both good for you and the company to monitor progress and results. However, it is always a good idea to keep track of your own data outside of a company computer for your own benefit, and for the future, which may include a sudden or unexpected departure from a company.

You should be doing in-depth research on your prospects and keeping it in your own system for your own benefit. Again, a task made far easier by the Internet, Yahoo, and Google. Make notes immediately after each call, and record all information from each day at the end of each call. If you wait a day or week to do this, human nature is that you will forget half the important facts, and the likelihood of you going back to do it is reduced by 90%. Be sure you use your system to track dates for reminders of follow-ups. You have the benefit of technology, so use it your advantage.

In addition to providing existing account records in your territory, some companies also provide a list of closed accounts, and sometimes even leads, while some will expect you to do all the prospecting and lead generation. The general rule is, the more they expect you to do, the larger the commission and the higher the potential earnings. It is important during the interview process with a potential employer to determine just what the company will provide in these areas as well as what will be expected of you. Get it in writing! Recruiters and Sales managers are usually great bullshit artists and great at selling their own agendas, which may not be in line with your best interests.

Without a concentrated effort on organization <u>every day</u>, you will fail <u>every time</u>!

Chapter Seven:
Checking Out Your Prospective Employer

This is a priority; always check out your future employer! Do this thoroughly, or don't do it at all, as if you don't, everything else will have been a waste of time. There are a number of ways are available for you to do this, which is the same way any reputable company should and likely will check out your background. The primary source for you will be the internet.

1. DUE DILLIGENCE: Pull a stock report on the company if it is public, easily found on the Internet. If it's a private company, ask for references. You may be reluctant to do this, but if it's a good company, what have they got to loose? Any smart company will respect you for asking. Check job bulletin boards on the Internet as well as sites like "TheVault. com" which offer detailed reports on companies and company culture, however, remember that even with reliable sources, sometimes people have an axe to grind, so go to plenty of sources, and go with the majority of the information that is consistent from the reliable sources.

2. SALES MANAGER: Request to meet your future Sales manager, this is a must. Size them up, just as they are sizing you up. Remember that's the person who will become the most important person as it relates to your relationship with the company. Does he/she impress you? Ask questions as to their ideas on selling and managing. Make up a list of questions relevant to the products/service, your territory and its history, your job requirements, how many Salespeople preceded you and for what period of time.

3. TOOLS: Ask what Sales tools the company will supply you with, such as; Car, Laptop computer, cell phone, Sales software, what expenses are paid, office supplies, tuition reimbursement, benefits, health insurance, stock options, matching 401k, etc.

4. TRAINING: You will want to know about the entire program in detail. How often will there be training, who will be running the program (a manager, an executive, a trainer, a consultant), over what period of time will it take place, and what does the training consist of. Large corporations will have a Training Manual and/or Sales manual, so ask to see it. Ask about field training; how much time will your Sales manager spend with you in the field making Sales calls?

5. GET IT IN WRITING: Get it all in writing before saying yes or signing an employment agreement or ANY document. Also, be careful of non-compete clauses if you plan on staying in the industry. Check state laws (available at most state department of

Labor websites) on non-compete agreements, and ALWAYS have a lawyer review any contract or agreement before you sign it (trust me), or you could live to regret it. Any company worth working for will respect your thoroughness.

Sound tough? You bet. You are making one of the most important decisions in your life, so isn't it worth the time and effort to be as sure as you can be? Get as much information as possible, as you don't want to make a mistake you will regret, one that will cost you time and money.

CHAPTER EIGHT:
PRODUCT KNOWLEDGE

In telling you about Product Knowledge, let me first tell you how it should not happen. Once again, my first Sales job is a great "bad example".

The field training in my first Sales job was fairly good; the first week in the field with the Sales manager, the second week alone, the third week in the field with the Sales manager again, the fourth and fifth week alone. But there was a problem; my manager only spent 30 minutes in total out of all of that time on product knowledge.

My company operated on the sink or swim theory; if you survived long enough, you would eventually figure out what you were doing and what you were selling. That theory was a very costly one, and amounted to a 75% annual turnover rate nationally in the Sales force. Gerry, my Sales manager, was a great Salesman and an excellent manager. He followed the company policy, which was to get Sales when he went out with me. That was how I was supposed to learn, by example. While that was great for selling, it was not so good for learning anything if you didn't know the first thing about the product you were supposed to be selling. This was pretty basic and pretty stupid in my opinion, but this was 1950's & 1960's thinking, and you didn't contradict your manager or your company back then – you had to be a team player. The problem was, I realized very early on that Sales was not a "team sport".

Despite the obstacle, I quickly learned through my secret weapon; desperation. I was quickly closing 3 to 4 Sales a week using the Sales kit and by having memorized one of my manager's presentations and closing pitches I was doing well. The problem was I still had no idea what I was doing. I was doing it all based on pure adrenaline, desire, and stick-to-itiveness. I was lucky at this point, as I had the Regional Sales Manager working with me too, which compensated for the half ass one week product training at the home office.

The moral of this story is that poor product training can hurt your ability to sell and thereby handicap your ability to make money, so you need to make sure the company you choose has a great program. However, even in the worst of circumstances, there are always people who are successful, despite a myriad of obstacles.

Though my company by far had the best product in its field, it was always number two. The reason? Poor product training and too much emphasis on new sales, and not enough emphasis on existing customer sales. Again, this is the sink or swim method of doing business, and it doesn't work in the long run, nor does it make for a successful company or a successful Sales force long term.

Be sure it doesn't happen to you. Check out the Sales and product training of your future company carefully and ask a lot of questions.

IN YOUR SECOND INTERVIEW ASK THE
HIRING MANAGER FOR:

1. The Sales training manual (you may have to review it onsite)
2. The product training manual, if there is one (also, may be restricted to onsite viewing)
3. A Schedule of class room training and what it comprises
4. How much time is spent on product/service training each month?
5. What support is available via phone or computer to back you up?

This is not the time to be shy, your future is on the line, so don't be afraid to ask questions, and if you don't like the answers, or something doesn't seem right or sound right, then you have your answer.

Chapter Nine:
Telephone Techniques

Use a Sales script; this may sound corny and old fashioned, but having a script or even an outline in front of you when you are making calls for appointments is a smart move and a great confidence builder, especially if you have never used the phone for securing appointments, or you are new to the product. The company may provide you with one, which is a great starting point, however, if not, make one up yourself.

Use the phone to your advantage and make maximum usage of your time by seeing the right people. Don't waste time on assistants, secretaries or others who can't make decisions and sign on the dotted line.

What is your goal in making the call? Verify you're talking to the decision maker and get a firm time and date for an appointment. The purpose of your call is to get the appointment and not get into a conversation, which if you do, I can guarantee you will lose almost every time, which means that you will end up without an appointment. What will you end up with? One of these excuses; "Send me literature", "Call my assistant", "Call me in a month", all put offs.

I used this basic presentation and script over 40 years with various changes, dependent on the product or service.

EXAMPLE:

Good morning Mr./Ms -----------. I understand you are in charge of purchasing----------. I've called several times but have not connected with you. I'd like to get 10 minutes of your time on Tuesday, November 22nd, at 10:00am. Or perhaps Thurs, November 24th at 2:00pm is better?

Now, if you got the date/appointment, shut up and get off the phone! You closed and the next words are up to the person on the other end of the phone. You talk, you lose. Make no mistake, every call is a win or lose situation, and all are a possible win. If the answer is yes, simply say, "Thank you Mr./Ms. --------, I'll put it in my calendar, please do the same, I will see you Tuesday at 10am", and then hang up. No conversation.

When you make up that telephone script or outline, or you are given one by your company, make sure you have the responses to the various questions, objections, or excuses you may encounter so that you can provide a comeback quickly.

If the answer is, "No, it's not convenient", then have your comeback ready; "How is Friday, November 25th, at 1pm? Or, how about Wednesday, November 30th at 3pm?". Eventually someone is going to give up, and as long as it isn't you, and you keep coming back with alternative dates and times, most of the time you will win and get the appointment. I have many times gone thru 4 or 5 dates before I received a yes.

When you are asked what the appointment is about? Simply respond that it is a new idea on xyz, dependent on what it is you're selling, and then immediately ask, "How is 10am Tuesday?

Have a script with the half dozen most likely major objections written out with your responses in front of you for at least the first six months. It's a security blanket and allows you to lead the combat. And make no mistake, it is combat, and in combat, someone wins and someone loses. Be the winner! Be prepared!

Since the person you are calling doesn't know you, don't take the rejection personally. How can it be anything but impersonal. Once you get past and get over the fear of rejection, and make no mistake it is a FEAR, (it is human nature to fear it) then you are on your way to being number one.

In my very last career change, it took me almost two years to get my first large order. I made 100 cold calls every day starting at 8am and did so non-stop until 6pm. My market was Attorneys of large Manhattan Law Firms, Investment Bankers, and Presidents, CFO's., and General Counsels of corporations. I can not think of a tougher group to have as prospects. I heard "NO" 98 times a day, and when they say no, they mean it. With all the success I had in previous jobs using the phone to get appointments, never had I run into anything like this. This was the 80's in New York City.

I made a decision early on; either they were going to break, or I was, but I wasn't going to break, and I knew it. Well it worked, and trust me, it will work for you. Just remember that every call is win or lose, and persistence and patience wins every time.

Cold calling can be fun if you don't take it personally. Get over the fear and remove the biggest obstacle to your success in

Sales......FEAR. Once you have removed it, and only you can remove it, you will be on your way to being number one!

OVERCOMING RESISTANCE

Always have a fast response to the objections, it is the key to you getting in the door, as well as the first impression the person on the other end of the phone will have of you. Quick, precise, and hard to argue comebacks will leave the impression on your prospect that you are smart and good at what you do. After you've sold for just a few weeks you will have heard them all, so write them down and work them all into your script. Remember you have the upper hand, as you're the one with the script. If you really are prepared you will have an answer for almost any objection that a prospect can raise.

SOME EXAMPLES OF OBJECTIONS YOU MAY RUN INTO IN YOUR CALLS:

Prospect: *"Send me some literature"*

Your Response: *"Nothing we have at present adequately gets to the points that I want to discuss with you in detail. In ten minutes, I can do that more efficiently. How is Wednesday at 11am?*

Prospect: *"Now is a bad time!"*

Response*: "I understand you are busy, but I just need 10 minutes at 11am on Wednesday, and that will give you the complete picture! Is that good for you?"*

Prospect: *"Call me back in 2, 4, or 8 weeks."*

Response: *"Since we both work on planned schedules, how is Friday the 26th, at 9am for just 10 minutes?"*

Remember, close them and then shut up! Getting the meeting and getting in front of them is your first stage of the close. Once you have a "yes" or an "ok", do not say another word! Reconfirm the time and date and get off the phone immediately. The first one who talks after that moment, loses.

In my experience this is how it is done in order to achieve the highest percentage of results. The more you talk, the more you lose. I have used this for over 40 years from rotary phones to cell phones, to IP phones, to smart phones, and over a five decade and two generation period, and it has worked consistently and without fail.

Of course you have to adapt these examples to your individual situation, personality, and product. No two people and no two products or services are the same. Yes, it's boring and exhausting, but the methods are proven, as are the results, which are big piles of money.

Maturity and dedication is what gets you motivated to do this day in and day out; there just isn't any great secret or magic pill. Over time and through repetition you will get better, and as you get better, your confidence will grow, and as your confidence grows, your close ratio will go up, and as your close ratio goes up, you will make more money. Isn't that what it's all about?

CHAPTER TEN:
PRESENTATION

Have you ever heard the old joke, "How do you get to Carnegie hall? Practice, practice, practice!". Well, the same is true in Sales, except the only way to get good without killing off thousands of good prospects is to have a partner to role-play with. If you go to work for a large firm chances are you will get to role play and be video taped. Then someone will review it with you and critique your presentation. Unfortunately most small to medium size companies do not have these programs as part of their training program. If you end up at such a company, be creative; first find your role playing partner. In my case it was my wife. Second, make up a list of objections you have heard and work out good responses. Next use your web cam or home video camera (most handheld digital cameras shoot video) and practice!

Plan a two hour session at least once a week, as the more you practice, the faster you will see results, and results are closed Sales, and closed Sales are MONEY! Review the videos with someone else you know in Sales whom you admire and respect and between the two of you, you will see the weaknesses. The more you do it, the faster the payoff. Consider it a cost of doing business. This is the best investment you will ever make in your Sales career, it will return results a thousand fold.

If you go to work for a large corporation they will have a Sales manual with the presentations all neatly laid out with class room training, video sessions, etc. The question is, is this a big bucks job – six figures a year? If you are being put through the ropes from scratch, usually not, as these are set up for inexperienced or first or second job Sales people (less than 5 years experience) and the earnings potential is usually reasonable, salary plus commission or bonus. If that's what you want then it is a great place for you. If you are going to put yourself on the line with the goal of making a lot of money, then in most cases it will be a straight commission job or Commission versus Draw, with far fewer advantages, perks, and niceties, one of which is training.

The Product

If you aren't in love with the product or service you are going to sell, you need to realize something important; SELLING IS NOT ABOUT LOVE, IT IS ABOUT MONEY!!!

Check out the company and product that you will be selling. Is the company reputable? Is the product well thought of? Perhaps it's not number one in its category, so try to ask users what they think. Be creative and do some research. Locate prospects and users of your potential employer and competitors and draw up a list of questions. Get on the phone and ask them the following questions:

1. How did you buy this product or service?
2. Why did you buy this product or service?
3. When did you buy it and what were the terms and/ or price?

4. What is your satisfaction level with the product or service?
5. Why didn't you buy another brand or service?

Make it short and sweet, not more than 90 seconds. Then, the last and most important question, **"would you buy it again?"**

If you care about your future and you want a good idea where your potential employer and their product/service stands in their market place, you owe it to yourself to check it out, so invest three or four hours in your future. The majority of people will be responsive to your survey. Give it a try, what have you got to lose?

CHAPTER ELEVEN:
CLOSING TECHNIQUES

If you are still with me, you now have the information to find a great company to work for with a great product or service, and you also know how to get in the door and get your first face to face appointments. So now we get to the hardest part for most Sales people, closing. This is especially true when you are calling on people who are older than you and far more senior on the corporate ladder than you are.

Let's face reality and deal with this fact right now; everyone you are calling on is higher on the corporate ladder than you are! You're a Sales person, and in the eyes of most of the people you will be facing you are at the bottom of the pile, or perhaps even UNDER the pile.

Try not to take this personally. Look at it rationally; the only real difference between you and your prospects is age, and perhaps a little more or slightly better education, and a few more toys. You have to develop a shell and a hardened attitude, which means you need to have a thick skin and hide your emotions. Think of it this way, you are smarter, more interesting, and know far more about what you are most certainly going to sell them than they do. If you sell that idea to yourself you have leveled the playing field. This is the single greatest problem with most Sales people – confidence. If you lack confidence and feel inferior to your prospects, it will show, and you will be at a disadvantage before you ever start. Be confident and never walk in a room feeling inferior to anyone!

I spent 25 years calling on Investment Bankers, Lawyers, and Corporate Executives, all of whom were better educated than I was. Early on I took the attitude that in fact I was smarter, more interesting, more successful, and knew more about the needs of the people I was facing, even though most of the people I was facing made anywhere from one million to several million dollars a year, and had advanced degrees from Ivy League schools. And you know what? It worked! In fact, in many cases it was I who looked at them as inferior, with many exceptions to that of course.

After I began my last career at age 48, within a few years I was in fact more successful, made more money, and had more toys, than most of the Bankers, Lawyers, and Corporate executives I was facing, but I never had to say anything about it or brag, I think they just sensed it, and more importantly they sensed my happiness and my confidence, and with that, I was on even ground and gained their initial respect, as well as my first foothold towards gaining their trust, respect and being viewed as not only one of their peers, but someone who could help them. You must do the same, and perhaps the best way is to start out by looking at them as equals and no less.

Remember the number one Sales person in most organizations is probably earning as much or more than almost all of the people they are calling on, no matter who they are calling on, including the CEO. There are many Sales people that I know and have worked with who have made high six to low seven figure incomes per year. Once you achieve this goal, then you can have the toys. That can be you! The question is, do you want it bad enough?

If the answer is yes, you do want it bad enough, then you have to learn to "close".

This is the first close line I ever learned from my first Sales manager Gerry more than 40 years ago. I have altered it slightly to make it more generic.

EXAMPLE -- SET UP FOR THE "CLOSE":

You: *"If I could show you a way to save xx% (or xx dollars) over the next year by using my product/service versus my competitors (your current product/service), wouldn't you agree that it makes sense to use mine?"*

After you had said your pitch, SHUT UP! Silence is golden. Look the prospect directly in the eye – and as I have already said, **the first one who talks loses**! Make no mistake; it IS about winning and losing. Based on the response you get from your prospect, you will know where to take the balance of the presentation, as if the answer is yes, don't say anther word, take out the contract or your computer and start writing/typing up the order.

EXAMPLE - FINAL CLOSE

You: *"Wouldn't you agree that this is something your firm should no longer do without?"*

"Doesn't this make sense Mr./Ms. Smith?"

The same rules apply to closing as they do to getting appointments on the phone; after you get a "Yes" or "OK", shut up and get out the contract. If the answer is yes, start writing. If its no, then your next response should be: *"What is it that is standing in the way of you committing to this?"*

How many times do you try to close? Until they push you out the door -- keep going. It doesn't matter what you are selling. Try to close on the first try, but if the answer was no, what do you have to lose? Nothing of course, you only have something to gain. This is the most effective method I have ever used, and I have sold both products and services. Very few people can't be sold on the first try if you're talking to the decision maker, and that's the key – make sure you are talking to the decision maker. Regardless of which questions you initially ask the prospect, you have no way of knowing which ones may work on the first close attempt; trust me, I have been surprised more times than I can count.

Some Sales situations require a written proposal be submitted, which is usually the case when you get into big ticket Sales, but most products and services do not fall into that category, so a quick close is usually possible. I am willing to put my forty plus years experience up and say my system will win every time. If you doubt it, try yours and then try mine and compare. That's a challenge if I have not yet made you a believer.

I am not trying to portray this guide as the Holy Bible, or the "Whole Bible", instead, think of it as one book within the Bible. No one book could possibly cover all the inn's and outs of selling, it's too complex a subject, so I am trying to hit the high points in a practical manner. Look at it this way, if you get just one or two good ideas or concepts that work for you, then it was time well spent.

CHAPTER TWELVE:
PERSONAL APPEARANCE

In my career I have met a lot of unattractive Sales people. Sure it sounds funny, and perhaps a bit mean, but it is just the truth. Some of those people were great Sales people, however many detracted from their Sales by their appearance, and could have been even more successful had they paid attention to one of the most obvious and simple things; their own appearance.

The fact is, God made some of us beautiful, some of us ugly, and many more of us average. That's reality, and it is hard to change, though perhaps today it is a lot easier to change your appearance than it was 30 or 40 years ago. The reality is, most of us fall somewhere in between, and though looks are not the key to success, appearance and presentation are very important.

For instance, shake hands with someone and you often notice their nails are dirty and uneven. The same goes for suits, shirts, skirts being wrinkled or ill fitting, or shoes being un-shined. The old saying is, cleanliness is next to godliness.

No one wants to do business with a sloppy looking Sales person. This is something you can control. For my first Sales job I only had two suits, but they were always clean and pressed.

You don't have to be rich or have a Hollywood wardrobe to look neat and presentable.

Hair should be well cut and neat. The style is up to you, but the objective is not to be a "peacock", and to not stand out in a crowd and to be perceived as different. Like it or not, first impressions are important, and they can help you or hurt you, so don't do anything to hurt that edge. Keep your body art and other body piercings covered up, and, leave the earrings, nose rings, or other piercings at home and for the men, keep your face clean shaven or your beard neat and trimmed.

> *My son, who worked at Lehman Brothers as a Vice President has more tattoos than most bikers. The ones on his right arm stretch from his shoulder and around his arm half way down his forearm. They aren't cartoon characters either. He also has five piercings in one ear from his teenage years. However, in his years at Lehman brothers he never once rolled up his sleeves nor did he let anyone know he had tattoos or that he rode a Harley Davidson and ran with a rough crowd. He kept his personal business to himself.*

Once they have looked you over, then the rest is up to you. Don't allow something silly to sidetrack your career. Show your individualism on your own time; during the day, the idea is to not allow someone any excuse to not like you or not buy from you.

Ask a friend or significant other for their honest evaluation. If they hesitate, you need to re-evaluate and clean up your act!

CHAPTER THIRTEEN:
LANGUAGE

I hope that people of many different backgrounds and nationalities, as well as different education levels will read this book. This brings to mind the simple fact that everyone is different, whether it be because of where they grew up, where they went to school, what their parents did for a living, their socio-economic background, or dozens of other factors.

One of the first things most people notice after someone's appearance is the way that they speak. It is the most noticeable difference in people after their appearance, and likely the second thing that people will judge you on after you walk in the door. The differences fall into several different categories:

1. Tone
2. Accent
3. Vocabulary
4. Grammar & Usage

The good news is you can change 3 out of 4 on the above list. The first, tone, is something you are born with, and while with a good speech therapist you can affect even tone, it is numbers 2 – 4 that are really important, and ones that you can change and that will be the primary basis for how you are perceived not just by prospects and clients, but by almost all people you encounter.

Accents tell us a lot about people, in some cases it tells people where you are from, and in others it can be an indicator of your socio-economic background. In extreme cases, an accent can blur and distract from what you are saying and make it difficult for a prospect to understand you.

An accent can sometimes be a benefit, and in other cases a hindrance. It has been my experience that anything extreme becomes a distraction from your message. In most cases you will never know what is going through someone's mind, so the idea is to try and remove any potential obstacles.

Here are some tips on speech that I have found work well:

Avoid using regional terms not widely known

Concentrate on your speech and keep your accent to a minimum. If necessary, use a tape recorder or video recorder to practice reading and then have someone else listen to it and critique it

Avoid using slang

Avoid using profanities, even if your prospect does

Avoid using more words or larger words than necessary to convey your message – in most cases you won't impress anyone, and it will be obvious you are trying to do so, which will work against you

After you have mastered control of your speech, the next two very important things to remember are, **silence is golden** and **think before you speak**. This means put your brain in gear before you open your mouth. There is nothing wrong with taking 3 or 4 seconds after the introduction while you are getting settled to think about what you're going to say, but there is nothing worse and nothing more awkward than watching someone speak and hearing their speech peppered with what I call "Stumbles". This is a list of things that you should consciously avoid while speaking, and generally you will find that the primary cause of stumbles is either, lack of preparation, nervousness, or lack of confidence:

AVOID THESE STUMBLE WORDS:

1. "Like….."
2. "And a…."
3. "You know….."
4. "And Uh…."
5. "Umm…."
6. "But…."
7. "Well…"
8. "So…"

These are not only stumbles, but fillers, and they are immediately noticed, and generally looked upon unfavorably by your prospect, particularly when they are used repetitively, which is usually the case. Constant use of these terms throughout your speech will not only turn off and distract your prospect, but it will tell him that you are not prepared and not number one. If you can't speak well then you are never going to be number one, and it is one of the major causes of failure in Sales, and directly tied to preparation and confidence.

Look for these terms in your speech when you videotape yourself. Eliminate the hems and haws in your speech, and if you think your language is below the standard that you need for your Sales position, take a course in public speaking. There is nothing to be ashamed of, and most of us could benefit from such a course. Courses in public speaking give you good feedback from your fellow attendees and instructors, and also help to build confidence and help you to overcome the fear of speaking in front of others without the risk of doing it in front of a prospect.

In my career I have been through many different training programs that ranged in length from one day to two weeks. No matter how good you think you are, you will always pick up a new idea or viewpoint during one of these training programs. Some of the programs I took were after I had been in Sales for 25 or 30 years, and even after that much time in the field I felt revitalized by some of them, as well as having revisited many basic points that I had either forgotten over time, or that I had stopped using.

> **TIP:** Take 15 seconds as you are getting settled in your prospects office to look around. You'll pick up any number of ideas and insights about them and their life, job, family, or hobbies, by looking at what's in their book case, on the wall, and on their desk.

Successful Sales is 80% you and 20% the product or service you are selling. I was never fortunate enough in my career to have ever worked for what I believed was the "Industry Leader" of the product or service I was selling, I was always the underdog. Instead of viewing this as a negative, it drove me to work twice as hard as the other guy, as I needed to compensate for the lack of status of my product or service, which made me self reliant. Towards the second half of my career it became clear to me that what I was really selling was ME. Unfortunately for me, this took me a while to figure out, but once I did, it changed my life, and I soon realized that my reputation was more important than the product, and that is what I sold – MYSELF!

CHAPTER FOURTEEN:
WORKING WITH YOUR SALES MANAGER

Sales Managers can be a major source of frustration in your job. God knows I have had many more bad ones than good ones over the years, but that is not to say that there are not plenty of good ones out there.

What kind of Manager you will end up with largely depends on what segment of management is running or driving the company; Manufacturing, Accounting, or Marketing and Sales. In many cases Sales and Marketing are two separate operations, which in my experience is not a good thing. Another factor is where the Executive management (The President and/or CEO) has his or her background; did they start in Sales, Finance, Operations, or Legal. All of these will be factors in how your company's Sales organization is set up and functions.

Most accounting, manufacturing, and marketing executives think Sales people are brainless and should keep their opinions to themselves and just sell. I have heard this many times over the years, "Just sell what we give you". Of course the people who say this usually never made a Sales call in their lives. In rare cases there will be executives who will actually want the

Sales persons input, but these are far and few in between, so don't hold your breath waiting for this scenario to happen.

Naturally every Sales manager will tell you, "My door is always open", but in my experience, this is lip service and bullshit. In 42 years in Sales I met two managers who actually did that. Another thing I found to be true amongst my Sales Managers, if it isn't their idea, it's not going far. That is unless they suddenly make it their idea (read: Steal your idea!), which I have also unfortunately experienced. However, maybe you will be one of the lucky ones and have someone in management who is looking for your feedback. If so, your company is probably not an American company.

Another common management tactic is to "deny, deny, deny". It's CYO (cover your ass) in most companies. Stop and ask yourself, why is American industry losing its power in the world? The answer is that companies in other countries are hungrier, more innovative, more agile, faster, and adapt quicker. An excellent example is the US auto industry, which over the last 30 years has lost its dominance through a failure to innovate, move quickly and listen to its dealers who are ultimately the sales people.

Understand your role at the beginning; it is to sell, and not to complain about the product or service you sell. Remember, I said in an earlier chapter to check out the company, its products, and its reputation. Once you are a part of the company your input is part of what will shape the company, assuming it is welcome. To cover your own ass, send emails to your manager with suggestions and ideas, but always do it on a positive basis. Emails leave a trail that proves you came up with the concept or suggestion. But remember, no whining or complaining, always put things in a positive light.

In the auto industry, the dealers have been telling the auto manufacturers for more than 30 years what is wrong with American cars, and what they can do to improve quality and gas mileage. In that time their Sales have been cut in half, and more recently by even more, and after 30 years, most are now on the verge of bankruptcy, and some are bankrupt, and a few are just now starting to listen and get the message. This is why I have two foreign cars. I'd love to buy American, but in order for me to do that, it has to make sense. My son owns an expensive American Motorcycle which cost as much as a new car. He loves that bike dearly, but even he is realistic and knows that what he is really tied to is the brand, and that he is tied to it with the understanding that the cost of his loyalty is frequent problems and expenses. As he often says when the bike breaks down, "If I wanted a bike that ran well, or even ran all of the time, I would have bought a Honda".

Study the marketplace before accepting a position; you may well avoid joining this type of company, one that doesn't listen to its employees, or the market. There are many smart companies out there who do listen, so do market research and remember that the company Sales force is the horse pulling the cart, so this likely means that a smart company has a smart, organized, and effective Sales force.

If you find yourself stuck at a company that is close minded or backwards in their thinking and perhaps heading in that direction, get out, and get out quickly. You, as a single Sales person will never be able to change the company or the situation. Things are changing so fast in technology that in one year your product or service is the best, and the next year another company has usurped you and you are no longer the dominant force. Market research is now a necessity for every company in order to stay ahead or at least be competitive. It is also a necessity for you, whether you are in search of a new Sales position, or competing in the market for new Sales.

Know your company, but know your competitors even better. The same is true in life in general.

Overall, this is an argument that has no end, and I present this to you so that you are aware that a career in Sales is no bed of roses.

Many years ago I was in a Sales representative for a company who had a similar mindset to the auto industry. Any new Sales person knew within a month that they were working for the number two company in the industry because management refused to listen to the people who were selling their products. Unfortunately I stayed for 10 years, which was a huge career mistake. You would have thought the tip off would be the 75 % annual turnover of Sales reps! But instead, the company blamed it on the Sales people. Those of us who stayed and survived learned to sell around the weak points in the service. That's not ideal in any Sales situation, and not something you should try to do. Had I moved on as I should have, who knows where my career could have gone, and perhaps I could have retired 10 years earlier. Don't make the same mistake. When you spot a landmine, don't try to walk around it or defuse it, run in another direction to safer ground!

Dependent on your relationship with your Sales manager, and how flexible he/she is, will determine how you communicate with them. If you have a real old fashioned "company man/woman" for your manager, one who believes the company can do no wrong and is always right, then you are in for trouble. Do your best to limit your communication to reports and facts. Keep your head down, stay clear of conflict and confrontation, and do not rock the boat with criticisms and ideas on how the company could improve the product or service. Trying to change things will only cause you grief and end up with your being branded "difficult" and a "trouble maker", and in the end you will become frustrated, and your performance and your compensation will be affected.

On the other hand, if you are fortunate enough to have a open minded Sales manager, express your thoughts in a more open and honest manner, but be careful not to assume to much or to become to comfortable. Familiarity breeds contempt, and also problems. In other words, no matter how much you may like your manager, or how much he/she may like you, don't get too close. It is important to always remember that <u>your manager is not your friend</u> – he/she is your boss, and you need to be careful to keep it cordial and not get too personal. Keep your personal life and your personal feelings and problems to yourself.

> **TIP:** Prior to accepting a new position, request to meet your direct Sales manager and ask all of the questions mentioned in Chapter 7. If the company will not allow you to meet the manager prior to accepting the job, then you should not accept and move on….. this is the first sign of many bad things to come.

CHAPTER FIFTEEN:
LOYALTY

Times have changed dramatically from when I started selling. In the 1950's and 1960's company loyalty was the most important thing to employees. This represented people's need to feel like they were a part of something bigger, and the notion that companies were like families. After you had been with a company for 4 - 5 years, you were hooked and you hoped and expected to stay for 30 years, get a dinner, a gold watch, and perhaps a pension. Those days are long gone. Back then almost all Sales people wanted to feel wanted. An American management association survey I read back in the 70's said that a survey showed among Sales people that the number one priority for employees was, "wanting to be part of an organization".

Things are vastly different today, and it isn't uncommon for someone to have three to five jobs in a five year period. Strangely, this is no longer looked down upon, and is simply considered the norm in our fast paced moving society. However, it is my belief that people leave companies for a few simple reasons, chief among them because they aren't treated well, and/or they aren't treated fairly.

While in many disciplines people also move around because they feel that it is the best way to keep moving up the ladder, this notion works the complete opposite way in Sales. You will never be number one or a top earner in any big ticket sales job if you don't stick around for at least two to three years in each job. Any good Sales Manager will spot a job hopper and quickly deduce that this person has never been anywhere long enough to produce or show top notch results.

What would you rank as your top five career priorities? Sit down and make up a list. You may be surprised at the results!

1.

2.

3.

4.

5.

After having read this far, you should now know a fair amount about yourself if you are being honest with yourself. What I have said is merely a review of the facts and the options. You're the one who has to determine who you are and where you think you fit into the big picture.

Is a career in Sales really for you?

CHAPTER SIXTEEN:
IS A CAREER IN SALES RIGHT FOR ME?

I am sure you have come up with a list of questions and thoughts of your own by this point, so here are few that I would guess you might have:

1. **Is this guy nuts?**

   Nope, just up front and realistic about the facts, which in case you haven't noticed, aren't always pretty – but that is reality and life – not always pretty.

2. **Does this guy have <u>anything</u> positive to say about being in Sales?**

   If you read carefully, you would find that I did in fact point out many positive points; however, there aren't a lot of them and it is a tough road if you want to be a winner.

3. **This guy was probably a failure in Sales who is just doing his own complaining!**

   Nope, every year for the last fifteen years of my career (1993 - 2007) I made between $300,000 - $700,000 a year in commissions (I retired in July of 2007), and at 74 years old I was the number one sales person at a billion dollar a year international company.

4. **Isn't his view of management distorted?**

   Not in my opinion; it is based on 42 years of experience at various companies that ranged from $20mm a year to Fortune 1000, and in my view it is simply very realistic.

5. **Is Sales really as tough as he describes?**

   If you want to be number one, absolutely!

As I said, the truth isn't always pretty, and my assessment is based on the cold hard facts and an overview of 42 years of encountering thousands of companies, meeting thousands of prospects, and thousands of Sales people. I assume you would like to be number one if you are going into Sales, but it is important to review your motives, and as I also said earlier, if the first three reasons are not money, I would question your decision. This is a profession that tests you every hour of every day, as its win or lose on every call, there are no draws, and there are no rewards for the loser. Sound tough? You bet it is, and that's why on average 90% of commissioned Sales people do not last 10 years in Sales.

Of course my way isn't the only way, but I think that if you look at any other really successful Sales people, others who are number one in their company or in their field, you will find most of the components I have mentioned are part of their repertoire, although they may be adapted to the individual, which is something that is important to remember; adapt these concepts to your life, your situation, and your needs.

Can everyone be number one at their company? The answer of course is no, but you will never get close unless you are willing to put out 110% every day. It takes that effort at the minimum to even hope to be at or near the top. Natural talent is always good, but in reality it is not that important. The fact is, most of us (including me) don't have it, so the only alternative is to learn it, and work for it, and that takes a 110% effort, 110% of the time. It worked for me and I was certainly average by anyone's standards, and the man I am today is totally self manufactured. Did you hear me? I did it myself. The companies that I worked for gave me an opportunity, but little else. This means that you can do it too. You just have to make the commitment to the learning curve, which for everyone is different, but realistically you can expect a one to three year curve for someone starting in their first Sales job with no experience.

There are no magic short cuts, and this isn't a late night infomercial promising you a get rich quick scheme from a guy whose only accomplishment was reading well from cue cards and good editing. This is from someone who has done it successfully for more than four decades and has the results to prove it.

So, if all of this is so obvious, then a logical question would be, why do 80% of all Sales come from 20% of the Sales force in most corporations? Because the 20% who produce are the ones who want it bad enough to put out the 110% effort in all of the areas I have outlined. Companies can not make you successful, only opportunity, discipline, hard work, and hopefully some training and a few tools will. Don't expect that your company or your manager are going to be replacing your mama and will take care of you. If that's what you need, go live with your parents. In Sales, you are it, period, just like in Golf or Tennis – Sales is not a team sport and there is nobody else to count on, blame or congratulate, except yourself.

CHAPTER SEVENTEEN:
CHOOSING THE RIGHT COMPANY FOR YOU

Assuming you have gotten this far in the book, you don't totally disagree with my philosophy, and I have not scared you away. My objective is not to scare you, just to make sure that you very clearly understand what the facts of life are with regard to selling in today's fast paced ever changing business world. Unfortunately the facts aren't always rosy.

Picking your first Sales job is the same whether you are fresh out of school or you have been working for many years in a non-Sales related job. The first thing you will need is a great resume, which should be about one or one and a half pages long. Hiring managers could be looking at hundreds of resumes and are not going to look through three or four pages. You have just a few seconds, perhaps fifteen to thirty, to catch the hiring manager's attention.

For those fresh out of college and entering the workforce for the first time, your education, extra curricular activities, and part-time jobs and volunteer work while in school should all be mentioned. Also mention your grade point average if it was exceptional (over a 3.0), and your job history, if any.

For those with prior work experience, don't leave gaps in time. Gaps guarantee questions or an automatic "pass", which means your resume goes into the garbage without you ever getting a chance to explain. Be reasonably honest about your past Sales statistics, especially anything you did that was exceptional or creative. Remember, <u>a good company always check references,</u> bad ones usually don't bother. NEVER give a reference that you feel might not give a wholly positive assessment, and always call your references ahead of time to ask their permission and let them know who may be calling, what they will be calling about, and what you hope they will say. Always ask the hiring Manager if they checked your references.

My advice is to draw up a draft of your resume and then have a resume professional or service re-do it. It may cost you a few dollars, but it is money well spent.

The first paragraph of your resume has to stand out and catch the reader's attention. If responding to an ad on the internet or in the newspaper, include a brief cover letter as to why you are qualified and interested. Remember, first impressions are important, but keep it brief.

I am not going to discuss how to handle an interview. God knows the library and Barnes & Noble have hundreds of books already written on the subject. I do however recommend that you read at least two books on the subject. What will impress many potential employers is how much you know about their business, and your questions will reflect just how much homework you did before the interview. Eye contact, posture, and body language will always tell volumes about you, so be aware of those and practice before you go in. A more important reason to be prepared is that a good interviewer will ask you specific questions about the company and product, and if you are not prepared you will not be able to fake it, and you will look foolish and worst of all, you will not get the job. Don't put yourself in this position, do your homework and BE PREPARED!

As I mentioned in an earlier chapter, doing research these days is a breeze with the internet, so don't be lazy; do your homework on the company, its products, and don't forget the company's competitors.

> **TIP:** If you can't find any information on a company using Google or Yahoo, then this is a major warning and RED FLAG! Any reputable small or large company will have anywhere from dozens to thousands of entries on a major search engine. Also, if you find consistently negative information, this is also a RED FLAG, and a sign you should move on and look elsewhere.

The Securities and Exchange Commission web site will let you look at annual reports and quarterly reports for any public companies for free. Also call a brokerage firm if you have an account and get a current research report.

Naturally if you can find someone such as an acquaintance or friend of a friend who might know someone who buys that product/service or works for the company it would be a great source of information. If it's a retail product go into a store and question the Sales person on what their thoughts are about the product and competitive products/services. Look at the packaging, contents etc., and you will be surprised what you learn.

In other words, check them out as carefully, just as they will likely check you out.

Managing your life

Draw up a budget of all your expenses, weekly, monthly, quarterly and annual, and include everything. You are going to come up with a number for each month, and that is the number that you need to base your life on. That number is the minimum you need to be sure you can make each month, unless you have a source of subsidy such as a wife or parent. Don't include business expenses, as any good job will cover those reasonably.

Now it is decision time. How much confidence do you have in YOU?

What kind of Sales job are you going to take?

1. Straight Salary (No Commission or bonus)
2. Salary + Bonus?
3. Salary + Commission
4. Straight Commission versus Draw (or perhaps no Draw)

We have already discussed what it takes to do the job, but what kind of confidence do you have in yourself? Take some time to think about that one, but remember, nobody ever got rich on a salary, and the safest option is usually the least lucrative one.

For the majority of the people who read this book, I would suggest taking option two or three for your first Sales job. Spend a few years learning the ropes and maturing. You'll know when you're ready for the big show, number four, which is where the real money is, but you have to be ready for it. You decide before the circumstances decide for you.

Back in college I knew a few people who were highly motivated and knew what they wanted. Most of those people succeeded in the long term, but they were among the few who were mature well beyond their years. As I mentioned previously, the majority of high school and college graduates have little idea of what they are going to do after graduation, let alone with the rest of their lives, with the exception of those going to professional schools, and those putting off reality for two or three more years by going off for an MBA. In most cases it is a case of too many parties and too little thinking about and planning for the future.

Most people spend the first few years out of school going from job to job without any direction until they happen to fall into one that is comfortable, not too demanding, and that will pay enough for them to get by. Are you the exception? Don't fall into that trap and let life happen to you! Wise up fast, as if you don't, it is a cold cruel world that's about to smack you in the ass!

Starting Over

I was forty eight years old when I changed careers for the fourth time and again took a straight commission job with a draw. It was 1981, and it was relatively rare at that time for a man to change careers so late in life. The company that finally hired me and took a chance on me told me that it could be a year before I made my first large sale. Unfortunately for me, it took closer to two years.

The President of my company at the time was an unusual guy who could see the forest through the trees, not always the case for men who have been successful and are in a position of power, and particularly at such a young age; he was 35.

Up to this point in my career I had always done well and I had been by most standards successful, but I was still not a good job picker, which was very costly for me.

I immediately went in the hole $48,000 in draw my first two years, and frankly most people would have called it quits and walked away to find another career, but I didn't. I stuck it out because I could feel it, and it was so close that I could taste it.

It turns out that I was right, as in my third year I not only made my draw, but I paid back my deficit and then some. From that year on until my retirement in 2007 (25 years), I went on to earn mid to high six figures annually – EVERY year.

The moral to the story is twofold. First, don't be stupid like I was and wait until you are 48 years old to pick the right job or even the right career. Second, all the factors I described up to now came together for me, but it took far too long. Learn from my experience and my mistakes; do your homework and go with your gut. Your instinct will rarely betray you, and your first instinct is usually the right one 99% of the time.

****

My belated thanks to Bob Rosenbaum for giving me a chance when nobody else would, and for taking a long shot on a 48 year old man with no experience in the industry. I like to think that he made the right decision, one that ended up benefitting us both tremendously. Bob truly deserves his own page

****

Chapter Eighteen:
Moving On.....Your Second Sales Job and Beyond

Now you have some experience and if things have gone to plan, you have now had your first Sales job for one to three years. Even if that is not the case, let's assume you have hit what you think is the ceiling at your current position, and you are ready to move on.

Evaluate Your Situation:

1. Did you earn above the average in your current/last position?
2. What were your reviews from management like?
3. Do you think you made the right decision when you took the position?
4. What are the short term opportunities to increase your earnings?

Give some serious thought to your results. Did you do as well as you could have? Are you up to a greater challenge and therefore feel you deserve greater compensation? You need to answer these questions and be totally honest with yourself.

Depending on what category your first job fell into, the answers to one or more of the above questions should guide you on what to do next.

Moving into Sales management, even if it's offered, is questionable. Not out of the question, but questionable. Making the move into Sales management involves a lot of responsibility, questions about what will happen to your compensation (it will usually go down if you were very successful in commission Sales), and significant travel in most cases.

Sales Management is usually not a good choice for someone with one to three years of Sales experience. Has it been done? Yes. Successfully? Rarely. If you are looking for management, my suggestion is to get a few more years of experience under your belt. Normally seven to ten years is recommended, and also the minimum that you will find most top companies are looking for. But why would you want to move into management? Your income will be solely dependant on the performance of others. Not a great choice in my experience, however, for some people it is the route they choose, and it works for them in their lives. Everyone is different, so, each to his own...

Someone who thinks he or she is the best and that they can go to the top of the Sales and earnings pile is not someone who will even consider management. If this is not you and you did not excel at your first Sales job, consider changing careers. Take a cold hard look at your results in your first few years. There is nothing wrong in recognizing that your talents may lie elsewhere. Perhaps you found that the type of Sales you were involved in is not suited to you. Selling products versus services requires a totally different approach and different set of Sales skills. You need to look at the time span and closing setup in different types of Sales, for instance, a one visit close sale versus a three to six month multiple presentation Sales cycle. Analyze where your interests lie and what your needs and expectations are and decide where you are most comfortable.

Let me throw out one idea for your consideration; a multi-call sale in many cases involves larger dollars and requires more negotiating skills. Not necessarily more money for you, but in some cases it may be if it's a high margin product or service. These are the variables that you need to consider. There are no easy choices and lots of questions. You will need to answer these questions for yourself before moving on to that second job.

CHAPTER NINETEEN:
SALES MANAGEMENT

As we touched on in the last chapter, the question is, do you want to be in Sales Management? This is a difficult question, and to the inexperienced, it may seem like a step up. Most inexperienced Sales people would say, of course I want to be a Sales Manager, it gets you out of the direct line of fire. However, it also puts you right into another line of fire...the corporate line of fire.

As I previously mentioned, I went into Sales management because I was coerced (Read: forced) and my back was against the wall; it was not my best choice or the decision I should have made. It's easy to be a Monday morning quarterback, but I can now safely say that I made a big mistake. If I was good enough to be number one in the national Sales force of a large corporation, I could have easily moved to another company with greater income potential, regardless of how precarious my personal situation was. I should have taken the risk, but I didn't, and I paid for it with years of my life and hundreds of thousands of dollars in lost potential commissions.

Sales Management was a losing proposition for me financially as it would be for any top earning Sales person. I made less money but built up a nice ego, however, ego does not pay the bills. Being a great Sales person does not necessarily make you a great Sales manager, just like being a great player doesn't make you a great coach. Most people foolishly make the decision based on ego and not money.

If you want to feel important, have an office, and push paper, be a Sales Manager. If you want to be rich, stay in Sales.

Being a Sales manager involves a lot of skills that must be learned, and like Sales itself, most of these things aren't taught in college. Things like recruiting, training in both the class room and in the field, report writing, evaluating performance, travel and then more travel.

Generally being a Sales manager involves more hours (and as we have already said) and less money (which we have also already said). If you have a family, this also involves them, as personal relationships are stressed from the time requirements and the travel. Giving up the freedom and potential financial rewards of being a field Sales person for a position where your hands will be literally and figuratively tied and where your future, for the most part, is not in your hands, is a decision you should weigh very carefully. Ask yourself is this is really what you want. These are the hard facts you face in moving into Sales management and attempting to move up the corporate ladder.

Ego and emotional rewards should be secondary issues, since you can't eat them, drive them, or live in them. Naturally we are all different, so perhaps your personality and goals are suited for management. For me, in the final analysis money is the best reward. Naturally, if the soothing of your ego goes with it, then it's all the better for you. We all have egos; just don't let yours run your life, a mistake easily made early on in your career, and one I made for a part of my career. Luckily mine finally worked its way out, and I got out of management before too much time was lost, but I wasted a lot of years and cost myself and my family a lot by not having woken up earlier and taken a different path sooner.

Be smarter than I was and make your decisions on hard facts. Investigate and find out what the rewards and benefits are and weight them out.

Generally in order to get ahead in management you need to be a great politician, not a talented Sales person or someone who has measured results. Unfortunately that isn't the way it should be, but the fact is, that is the way it really is in most major corporations.

If you do go into management and you turn out to be a very talented Sales manager, you have a 50-50 chance that your direct boss will be jealous of you and try and undermine you which is yet another hard fact of life, so be prepared to deal with it.

Weak management in American companies has been a problem for many years, and if you aren't in the right "fiefdom", you will quickly find yourself in trouble. There is an old Italian expression that I love; "The fish stinks from the head!".

CHAPTER TWENTY:
SALES EDUCATION....BE PREPARED

As I mentioned at the beginning of the book, I went to a mediocre University and majored in Business Administration, and to this day I have no idea what the point of the entire four year experience was supposed to be, or what I was supposed to have walked away with. Essentially, I learned nothing about the practical business world. The result was a lousy education, a worthless piece of paper, and no knowledge that prepared me for my ultimate vocation - Sales.

Unfortunately back then, and even still today, college classes are taught mostly by people who were never in the real world, and certainly you will not find many professors with any practical Sales experience. Today I assume that there are many more professors with real world business skills who have been successful, however, I would be willing to bet you still won't find many from a career spent primarily in Sales.

Today I recommend all young people get a good basic good Liberal Arts education that will help make you a well rounded person. Want a great business education? Go for an MBA at a top notch business school, as that is where you will come in contact with more of a real world approach, however, you still can't expect a Sales education.

Your best bet for a Sales related education is a private business school with successful Sales people as instructors, but unfortunately very few colleges and universities offer practical Sales courses. Why? I honestly don't know. You can get economics, marketing, and accounting, that are taught by successful business people, but not Sales related courses taught by a successful Sales person. In my opinion this is something that is really lacking in the American University system.

I often wonder what the purpose of a business school education is when millions of college business school graduates each year go directly into Sales, and without any real training or relevant skills. I have asked that many times, but I have not ever gotten a definitive answer. I have been told that there are a few schools around the country that have Sales programs, but I can't name one. Perhaps some day Universities will look on Sales as a profession and start a program in career Sales.

Going into a career without any training or education is like playing football with no pads, it doesn't make sense, and it can be painful.

I was told when I left college that being a doctor, lawyer, or accountant was a career, but that Sales was just something one does – just a job. Today I flatly reject that premise, and I now find that statement quite offensive, since as a Salesperson I made more money than most top Doctors, Lawyers and Accountants.

The insinuation is that professional careers involve special training and special skills, but not so for Sales. Baloney! Do most business people look down on Sales people? In my experience, for the most part, yes. Certainly many of the investment bankers, lawyers, and executives who were my prospects over the years did. My best guess is that they earn a lot of money and it's somewhat natural to feel superior. I never suffered from any insecurity because I knew I earned as much as many of them. Naturally in today's economy there are investment bankers who earn millions each year, so it is a little different, but they are in the minority. It is a state of mind and you have to sell to yourself and more importantly, you have to believe in yourself. I was lucky in that I always felt equal in all respects. Perhaps I was wrong and I really wasn't, but I believed it, so it helped me sell to these kinds of people and it was never a problem for me. Ironically, many of my long time friends ended up being my clients.

Given the narrow education and working environment of many of these people, I wouldn't trade places with any of the people I dealt with. The irony is that most people looked up to these exact same people and aspired to be just like them. However, my career in Sales lasted 42 years, how many investment bankers last that long in their industry? I would be willing to bet that very few have.

My very first Sales job was as a kid, and I was a *Fuller Brush* Sales person at the age of 15 in the 1940's. I would like to add that this company is still around today, more than sixty years later.

On my first day they handed me the samples, pointed me to the door and said go! Of course I failed miserably, but from that experience I learned quite a few lessons about what NOT to do, and I never forgot those lessons years later.

Remember, it's in your hands, so count on nobody but yourself and you'll always succeed. Your Sales education is in your hands if you use the tools I have outlined to help yourself.

If the word NO doesn't roll off your back like water off a duck, then you had better get used to it. Starting out, NO is what you will hear more often than your own name. A good response is, "can you tell me why you aren't interested?", or "What is it exactly that you don't see as a great benefit?". Always have a rebuttal. Hearing NO less frequently is directly correlated to your amount of experience and your success. Sorry, but there is no easy way.

CHAPTER TWENTY ONE:
COMPENSATION...$$$

As we discussed earlier, there is little to say about the word 'Salary" when it comes to Sales. There is no motivation that I can find that comes along with a salary, and there are also no rewards that come with it either. Why even bother being in Sales?

Salary plus bonus is the first acceptable level of compensation you should consider. In some industries a bonus can be a major factor such as in the securities industry, however, other than the securities industry, annual bonuses don't usually amount to much, perhaps 10% to 20% on average. The question of what will determine the bonus is the real factor, as if it is a factor out of your control, such as company performance, you should look elsewhere. Quotas should be clearly set out in writing. The worst kind of bonuses are at managements discretion; this should be self explanatory.....look somewhere else.

Salary plus commission is where it starts to get interesting. If the commission will represent a sizable portion of the total potential income then this is the kind of deal where you have a lot of incentive and no limit on how much you can potentially earn. You will need to know what the past history of your territory was, as well as what do the top Sales people in the organization currently earn, as well as how much of their total compensation was commission. Obviously you need to see all of the aforementioned in writing, though email correspondence is now considered acceptable. Be forewarned, most companies will not want to show you such records, but realize that if they won't, you should wonder why, as it is the roadmap to the journey you will be taking, and it also tells the story of the journey of those who came before you.

Draw versus commission, commonly referred to as, "a Draw", should be your goal after you have a few years of experience under your belt, perhaps 3 – 5 years. What this means is that you will receive regular payments (salary) in anticipation of, and against future commission. There are many variations of this, so you will need to look carefully at the agreement. Most important, always have an attorney licensed in the state that you are signing the agreement look at it before signing anything! Not doing so can be one of the biggest mistakes you will ever make, and one that could set you back for a year or more.

One variation of a Draw is that if you do not make your draw (earn as much in commissions as was paid to you in regular payments over the year) in the first year, you are responsible to pay it back out of your second years earnings. Most quality companies will forgive, or write off the first year deficit, and I would not recommend signing a deal where they will not and where the debt will accumulate, as you will likely never get out from under it.

Throughout the book thus far I have referenced my fourth and final career/industry change within Sales, and this was in 1981 in Financial Printing.

I was 48 years old and had no experience whatsoever in Financial Printing other than looking at the statements which were mailed to me each quarter from my 401k. I took the job on Draw Versus Commission. In hindsight, given my personal circumstances, this was not a wise choice, as it was a relatively small company, and because of my lack of knowledge of contracts at the time it was not made clear if the draw the first year had to be paid back or was to be forgiven. Sometimes not having a written agreement can work for you, but most times it will come back to haunt you and bite you in the ass. In my case, it bit me in the ass and I had to pay back the draw from future earnings, and it took me nearly two years to make my first large sale and get paid on it. It wasn't until that happened that I was hit with the information about the repayment of the accumulated draw debt. Was it Fair? NO. Even worse yet, another Sales person who had started 6 months prior to me never had to pay back a penny. Life is a bitch, and then you wake up. There was nobody to blame but myself, but instead of complaining, I realized I was onto something, and that I had hit the first vein in the mine, so I kept my mouth shut and soldiered on.

Because of my costly mistake, I cannot emphasize enough the importance of getting all of the terms of your compensation package, including benefits and any ancillary agreements, such as non-competes, <u>in writing</u>, and once again, have a lawyer from the state the agreement is being signed in review it. This is even more important when dealing with small companies (under 500 employees). Most large companies have an employee manual that spells out commissions, expenses, rules, and regulations, and larger companies are usually very good about documenting everything. The rule of thumb is, if you are not sure, ask, and get it in writing. Verbal promises and a token will get you on the subway, but not anywhere else......except a trip to the courthouse.

Large salaries for Sales people are very rare, with a few exceptions, such as those with many years of experience in a particular niche, and solid book of contacts and clients.

As I mentioned previously, the only salary plus bonus situation that I think is worthwhile in the long-term is in the securities industry. The bonuses in the securities industry are usually the major source of compensation for an experienced individual, and normally exceed the total salary many times over for those who are at the top of their game. The only problem is that very few survive in the industry, never mind surviving at a company for 10 or 15 years, as regretfully, turnover is extremely high. In today's world people move from company to company, often having 4 or 5 jobs in as many years with career advancement and increased earnings after each move. It has been a sellers/ employees market over the past ten years and top employees went to the highest bidder. As of the writing of this book, this is a different market, with changing market conditions which are rapidly deteriorating along with the Economy, which is currently in the midst of a major Recession, and perhaps the worst economic conditions in the last 70 years since the Great Depression. Thirty years ago it was exactly the opposite in the Financial Services industry, and I do not believe that in the long run either the industry or the individuals will benefit from how things have changed. Because of this, some institutions are now re-evaluating their methods of compensation and returning to the more conservative methods of the past.

After you have been successful in your second Sales position, you should now have three to five years of experience and you have hopefully been very successful, and put out 110%. If you have done this, then you are either a top producer or very close to it. If this is the case, then you are ready to go for the "draw versus commission". That's where the money is. Again, if it's not about the money, you're not mature enough or hungry enough for a career in Sales or you need to re-think your career choice. I say this with the greatest of concern for you and your future. Though it may sound harsh, the truth often comes off sounding that way.

Chapter Twenty Two:
Corporate Politics.....

I have never heard of a company where politics did not affect the business and exist in some form. In my experience *corporate politics* are one of the most destructive and disruptive influences in American industry in the late 20th and early 21st century, owing most of this distinction to the advent and rapid proliferation of cell phones, the Internet, and Social networks, all of which have increased peoples ability to easily, instantly and covertly communicate.

Starting in the 1970's I began to see the beginning of what would be known as *corporate politics*, which had at one time been something relegated to backrooms and boardrooms. It was about this time that I saw and felt it begin to come out of the board room and into the office, and rear its ugly head in many ways. Individual decision makers began to suddenly disappear and decision by committee became the norm. For me, this is what made selling more difficult over the past 30 years, as executives no longer made decisions alone. For example, the Vice President of Sales couldn't, and can't in most organizations today, make a decision that would change the Sales operation without months of discussions, committees, meetings, Board of

Directors approval, and perhaps in a large organization, dozens of people agreeing to the terms.

The corporate world today is all about power. In large corporations (FYI – a large company is one with more than 5,000 employees) relationships are key to your success and survival; the lesson being, stay close to the power. The trick is determining who has it, who wants it, who is scheming for it, and what exactly will they ultimately do to either keep it or get it.

So, you may be asking yourself, what the hell does this have to do with Sales? I thought I was on my own and the captain of my own ship? Well, so did I, until the following happened to me.

In 1974 I was a Regional Manager responsible for two hundred and fifty Sales people and eight District Managers. I was competing with another Regional Manager for top Sales honors company wide. The other Regional Manager was a protégé of the President of my division with whom I had no relationship whatsoever, and frankly whom I had little respect for and whom I had no interest in having any relationship with. The other Regional manager who suggested to the President of my division that my Sales people were writing questionable (Read: Fraudulent) orders. After an investigation, this accusation was proven to be totally without merit, and I then demanded that the same test be put the accusing Regional Managers Sales. Unfortunately he came up short, looking very foolish in the process, as both of us were responsible for reviewing all our Sales people's orders. This was the end of his climb up the corporate ladder, as soon after this incident he left the company, and not voluntarily.

How sure was I of the end result of that investigation? One hundred percent. I knew that when he had been a star Sales person his orders bounced all over the place and he became District Manager to escape the fallout. The moral to the story is that you need to be 100% sure of your facts before you pull out the knife, and when you do, make sure you are prepared to use it and that you are capable of finishing the job, or that same knife may be used to cut your own throat. Sadly, this scenario occurred more than once in my career. The real point of this story is to show what lengths many unscrupulous people may go to in their quest for the next rung on the corporate ladder.

My advice is simple; have real character and integrity, and demonstrate it every day. Be 100% honest in your work with your clients, your company, and most importantly with yourself. Never knowingly take an order or sign a deal/contract that is questionable without full management approval in writing, and get your manager to co-sign the order/contract. You always want backup in writing, as memories are short in the Sales universe.

Chapter Twenty Three:
Character, Ethics, Morals, and Integrity....

As I mentioned in the last chapter, you need to have real character and real integrity, and trust me when I tell you, neither is something you can fake. If you do fake it, you will quickly be exposed with disastrous results and consequences that can haunt you for the rest of your career.

You can always get another job, but once you give up your integrity, you can never get it back. It is the equivalent to selling your soul to the devil, so remember that. Your reputation is all that you really own in this world.

My character and my reputation are likely responsible for 90% of my success, and it is the one thing I held on to in 42 years of Sales, Sales management and Corporate management, and I held on to it with dear life.

I can honestly say with my hand on a Bible that I NEVER ONCE did anything in those 42 years that I thought was dishonest or that intentionally hurt my company or any one at the company. The only exception was if I was attacked, in which case I defended myself vigorously as I felt I needed to in order to protect and defend myself and my reputation, but I always did so cautiously and with the utmost integrity.

You can do the same, and no, it's not easy, but as I said before, once you lose (or in some cases, give up) your integrity, there is no going back. Even if you're the only one who will ever know, it is you who has to face yourself each morning in the mirror every day for the rest of your life.

Nothing I have achieved in my career makes me prouder than to be able to say to say to myself that I that I walked away from a 42 year career in Sales, and nearly 60 years of work experience with the same character and integrity that I started with. Believe me when I tell you it is something that makes you or breaks you as a person, and that you have to live with every day when you wake up and look in the mirror.

The question you need to ask yourself is, what do you want to see when you look in the mirror? The guidelines are very simple; your first instinct is usually correct, and if you think something is wrong or questionable, it usually is. The only question that remains is, what will you do when faced with a questionable opportunity? Remember, there are no shortcuts.

I think that perhaps in the 21st century the perception is that character and integrity are not such a big deal, and that cutting some corners where nobody will ever know isn't the end of the world, but trust me, in the final analysis, you will live to regret it, but by then, it will be too late to go back and do anything about it.

A reputation is something that takes a lifetime to earn, and only minutes to permanently destroy. It's like a piece of glass; in some cases it can be repaired, but it will never ever be the same and the cracks will forever show themselves in the light of day.

I want to be very clear that I am not trying to portray myself as saint, as I am not one, and by no stretch of the imagination am I perfect; no one is. There are many things over the years that I wish that I hadn't said or done, and we all make mistakes, and many are correctable, but some, those that compromise your character, are unfortunately not. Those are the flaws that will not only be evident to others, but more importantly, they will be evident to you, and you will rue the day you decided to take that shortcut and compromise your character, integrity and your reputation.

In the late 60's and early 70's the company I worked for had an unrealistic (Read: Tight) travel expense policy. This of course was one of several reasons why they were also the most profitable company in their industry. My food allowance was $8.00 a day, and $20.00 for lodging. Sounds like a joke today, right, but back then it was feasible, although even by the standards of the day it was tight. I traveled from Monday evening until Friday evening on an average of 48 weeks a year. Yes, literally 100% of the time. Since I was on a salary plus bonus, my earnings were well below twenty thousand a year at the time, and bear in mind that by 1967 I had a wife, a mortgage, and two young children. So, I ate one or two meals a day, the least expensive being breakfast and lunch, and I usually skipped dinner several nights a week as I was on the phone with my Sales force most evenings anyway. Remember, no computers or cell phones back then, so you couldn't communicate with your Sales force during the day. So, what did I gain from this? By scraping and saving all week, every Friday night I was able to take my wife out to dinner at a great local restaurant and celebrate the fact that WE made it through another week.

Was I cheating the system? Absolutely not; I worked within the allowance that was given to me and I never reported a day of travel that I wasn't actually traveling. A fool you might say? No one at the company would have known, so why didn't you just lie about your days and take the extra money and say you were traveling – who would have known? I would have known! And that my friends is the point, it is MY code of ethics. I tell you this because you will be faced with questions and temptations like this all of the time over the course of your career. We all have to make choices and live with them. What will YOU choose to do?

I hope that at the end of your Sales career you will be able to look back, feel satisfied, fulfilled, successful, and have no regrets.

CHAPTER TWENTY FOUR:
FINAL THOUGHTS ON THE EVOLUTION OF SALES, 1964 – 2010

The biggest change from the 1960's & 1970's to today is that cold calling (in person) is largely impossible in almost all major cities. With increased security in most buildings it is very difficult to get in without an appointment, whereas you used to simply walk in and go from floor to floor with a good chance of actually getting in to see the prospect without an appointment if you were lucky, but those days are long gone.

For many business services back then this type of cold calling or canvassing used to be standard operating procedure. However, I came up with a way around this that worked very well for me in many circumstances around the country, though **be advised, you should never break any local laws or disregard posted building security policies or rules.** Try making an appointment in a large building, and after the appointment cold call the rest of the building. You are already in the building, so do your homework ahead of time, and make use of the access and time.

The telephone was a great tool through the early nineties until voice mail took over and now few people answer their phone, and many never do, and simply use voice mail and Caller ID to screen all calls. In my opinion (and of course you know by this point I am a Salesman and prejudiced) these people are missing out on some of the best opportunities by prejudging and not talking to everyone who calls, no matter how briefly. Prior to voicemail you could easily get on the phone and in one day knock off 100 calls and book a weeks worth of appointments, which made for maximum effectiveness. However, this is sadly not the case today, and now even assistants and secretaries use voice mail to screen calls.

So what's a great Sales person to do? What's left? Email and Social Networks, which we will get to in the final chapter next.

From the 1960's through the late 1980's you could set appointments that were geographically convenient, which is not true today. With the tremendous increase in the pace of business, executive travel schedules have also increased. Time has become a commodity that is at a premium for most executives, and frankly at all levels of management. The higher up on the corporate ladder your product or service has to go to get the deal, the greater difficulty you will have getting the appointment. This leads to less productive travel and more time per Sales call, and thus far less face to face time per work week than there was even twenty years ago, perhaps as much as 80% less. I know that in some cases I have sold major deals (six figures) to people I had never even met, or I had perhaps only met once briefly. I often traveled to Dallas, Chicago, and California (well into my seventies) from New York for one hour meetings, and then immediately returned home, most of the time the whole trip taking 12 - 18 hours. Thought I was often physically and mentally exhausted, more often than not, I got the sale.

Today written hard copy communication is the weakest and least effective Sales tool available. Sadly, one percent responses in mass mailings are considered great results. Obviously don't count on this method to get appointments, though it is a way to introduce a new idea or product via an announcement prior to a call or email communication, but with the volume of junk mail most executives receive, in my opinion the chances are only 5-10% that it will get read if it is not an anticipated communication. While it cant be used en mass, Fed Ex and UPS are great ways of getting someone's attention, however, the cost adds up quickly, so it is something to reserve for those special or stubborn case where you think you might have the proverbial "White Elephant", and it is worth the cost.

Personal introductions and referrals are always the best way to get an appointment whether they are through alumni associations, friends, trade associations, etc. Join a local chapter of your High School or College alumni association and become active.

Looking forward, remember; NEVER make a sale without (after the sale, installation, or start of service) asking for at least three referrals. You will be surprised; it works most of the time. Catch the customer at their height of euphoria, just like you are right after you sign the papers to buy a new car – odds are you are at your height of confidence in the person you bought from, and a happy and confident customer will usually respond favorably. Similarly, a request to a fellow alumnus or trade group member will usually be met with a favorable response. Most people will recognize and appreciate your thoroughness and it will showcase your smarts, which most executives will respect. It will usually get you in the door and then the rest is up to you and your Sales skills!

Your Best Friend, The Telephone

Today, in order to get the number of live presentations you realistically need to be successful, you will have to devote a great deal of time to phone calls. This is a simple unpleasant fact. To give you an idea, I have found over the last several years that I needed to put in at least double the amount I was doing in the 70's and 80's. To me, in order to be successful, this means a minimum of 12 to 16 hours a week on the phone. If you do this religiously, in most industries this should secure you three full days of appointments.

As I mentioned at the beginning, have a script handy at the beginning until your confidence is built up. Yes, it's a crutch, but it is a proven one that works! Remember, you have the advantage! Your prospect doesn't have a script in front of them!

Always have a list of all of the possible objections and responses in front of you so that you can respond instantly without any hesitation. This is key!!!

The 21st Century & The Internet

Technology is changing almost daily, with new advances, new platforms, new software, new websites, and new companies. What does all of this mean to you? More tools.

The internet and software are tools, and like all things in life, some are good, some are not so good, and some are terrible.

I could write an entire book on this subject alone, however, there are plenty of them and they are written by people that are far more qualified on the subject than I am, not to mention that a good part of it is of no real importance to you on a business level in sales, so lets stick to the basics.

The good news is that there are now a handful of incredibly useful and valuable tools out there that you can simply and easily use to increase your sales. The bad news is that you need to use them correctly and not spend your time posting pictures of your Pet Rock collection to Facebook or chatting with your friends.

SOCIAL NETWORKS

Social Networks are just an accelerated version of our lives that we can view online. The good news is that Social Networks can expand our reach not only into our past, but into the future. The bad news is that there are dangers and pitfalls lurking for those that do not use them correctly.

As there are just too many to list here, I will give a few of my favorites that I believe to be most useful.

Facebook is a great tool, but it is rife with potential danger because the traditional perception is that of a personal social network. This means that people share private information about their lives, their families, as well as pictures and videos. I would recommend becoming VERY familiar, if not an expert, on the "Privacy Settings" and use "Groups" to separate business contacts from friends and family. Potential employers now also commonly scan Social Networks when screening prospective employees, so do this with caution, and make sure you are very clear on who can see what, and that the information your business contacts will see is appropriate.

One important thing to remember is that words on a page don't have intonation or facial expressions associated with them, and for people who don't know you on a personal level, those words may not have any context and can therefore often be misinterpreted. As with life, chose your words carefully!

Twitter is similar to Facebook in that it offers great opportunities as well as great danger. Be sure to have a separate Twitter account for business, and use it to provide your contacts with information that they will find useful, such as developments at your company, product developments, special offers or deals, or technology breakthroughs. The object is to become a wanted and reliable source of new and valuable information.

Linkdin is the de facto place for putting up your business contact information and connecting with others in a similar network style to that of Facebook. It is also an excellent place to find business contacts both through research and through your contacts networks. Its free version has always been suitable for me, however, it also offer various paid subscription plans which have more services and deeper information. While these plans are quite expensive, they may be suitable for larger companies, so ask your Manager if the company has a subscription, and if not, suggest they get one.

Hoovers is great source for corporate information as well as senior executives' names and titles. With the reach of Google and other social networks, Hoovers has become less important, though it is still valuable and should be your first source while looking for basic corporate information and executive names and titles.

EMAIL

Email in nothing new and has been common in the workplace since the 90's. However, using email effectively is still something many people have not mastered, and in many cases if you aren't careful it can be your downfall.

Many executives today prefer to communicate via email though in my opinion it is a very impersonal medium because it has a sort of finality and control to it, as it offers the potential to end a dialogue with no rebuttal from the other side (if they so choose). Later in my career as email became the standard I also found out that it was also an opportunity and that it could be used to my advantage. You should use email to make your message concise, hit the key points, and sell the meeting! Always request a face to face! That's your goal and your ace in the hole. Remember, even over email, the same holds true; "I am tied up on Monday", so the short answer is, "How's Tuesday at 10am for 15 minute?", or, "How is Friday at noon?". Don't take NO for an answer, and don't give up!!!!

Here is a common sense tip to start with; never send out email pitches to more than one or two people in the same company at the same time. Executives talk to each other, just like you talk to your colleagues. Doing this will diminish your response as well as your reputation. Spread them out over several weeks and move on to the next one once you have a response or determined you won't be getting one. Be persistent, but don't be a pest – it is a fine line.

Keep you messages short, 100-150 words, and make them to the point. Give as little information as possible, while creating enough interest to get a face to face meeting.

Don't send out mass emails, it simply isn't productive, and puts you on par with a mass marketing or Spam firm. In addition, if you do need to send out something to multiple people, use the "BCC" (Blind Copy), as executives don't want other people to see their email addresses or names. Send 20 or 30 emails a day, either early in the morning or late in the evening, and customize each email to the individual and the specific company – don't send out "Dear Sir or Madam" emails – you will be wasting your time and theirs. If you don't get a response after 2 or 3 attempts, don't keep sending to the same people, as it is irritating, just like it would be to you and they are immediately turned off before they ever meet you. Try to imagine yourself at their desk reading what you are sending and then try to put together something you honestly believe might make you respond. Be creative!

CHAPTER TWENTY FIVE:
TENACITY...

It was 1968. We had just moved from Philadelphia to the bucolic North Eastern New Jersey Mountain Town of Ringwood, New Jersey, where with a $3,000 loan from my company for the down payment, I had just built a new house for myself, my wife, daughter, and my one year old son.

Ringwood lies in the Ramapo Mountains on the border of New York State, just 40 miles outside of Manhattan. It was an up and coming area filled with new developments that housed young families willing to sacrifice a quick commute to Manhattan for the spacious inexpensive homes with fresh air, mountain views, and safe neighborhoods for their kids to run free through.

I had borrowed the $3,000 down payment from my company and built a two story colonial for $30,000. At the time I was making $12,000 a year, and it was a huge risk to say the least as I had just became a Sales Manager at my company, relocated, and went from a commission job where the sky was the limit, and where I was also number one, to my first Sales Manager job with a salary plus bonus. To make matters worse, I quickly found out upon my arrival in New York City that it was the worst performing district for the company in the whole United

States and that it had 28 open territories, not to mention the fact that it would be I who had to recruit all of the 28 sales people for those open territories, and do it quickly.

Our development in Ringwood was so new that the road had yet to be paved and the street was layered with gravel. This in itself would not have been so much of an issue just a minor inconvenience but for the fact that we were literally living two miles from the primary road, and our home sat at the peak of one of the steepest hills in Ringwood, with what I would venture to guess had a 30% grade, though don't quote me on that, but trust me, it was one steep hill. In addition, the main route in order to leave Ringwood and get into New York City was, and still is today, Skyline Drive, a precipitous, tortuous, and twisting six mile long two lane mountain road that has claimed many lives over the years, particularly during the winter months, during which it is notorious for closing during bad weather.

In February of 1969, New York City had what was at the time the 12th biggest snowfall in recorded history (which by the way goes back to 1798), 15.3 inches. However, 40 miles away in our little mountain town, it was 28 inches.

My friend Gary Bell, who was then in his early twenties had also just moved to Ringwood, and like most of us, he commuted to Manhattan every day. Gary and I had become friends and we took turns driving together to save money and to keep each other company. Gary was in a similar situation to that of mine; a wife, a baby, a house he could barely afford, and soon to have another baby on the way. Gary also shared my work ethic and my drive, something I had never encountered up to that point with any other man I had worked with or known, which was one of the many reasons that we became friends. Gary was also in Sales, and he was on commission at the time, so simply put; if he didn't make it into work, he didn't make any money.

There weren't even pushbutton phones at this stage, let alone voicemail, fax machines, the internet, or cell phones and smart phones. You needed to get to work in order to work and make money.

I awoke this particular morning at 6am to find that my front door would not open, as the more than two feet of snow that had fallen had drifted and was now nearly four feet high in front of my door, covering the bottom half of it.

I know that today the first reaction of most adults, regardless of age, would be relief and excitement; a day off! For me, it was different. It wasn't that I wanted to go to work; I NEEDED to go to work, and the only thing the snow meant for me was inconvenience and another obstacle I had to overcome in order to reach my goal.

I called Gary, who was already awake and thinking the same thing; lets get moving, its gonna be a long ride into Manhattan today!

So, we hopped into Gary's late 60's model Toyota Corolla, and off we went. Because he couldn't afford it, Gary did not even have snow tires, and there were no all-weather tires back then, so to say that the ride out of our development was frightening was an understatement. However, it was nothing compared to the terror of driving down Skyline Drive in what was essentially a car on skis with no brakes.

As we headed towards the city, we quickly realized that there was nobody else on the road – literally, not another car. As we slowly made our way to the George Washington Bridge, we were greeted with yet another and far worse obstacle, one which we had not anticipated. It was the the George Washington Bridge, and it was CLOSED. This is something that to the best of my knowledge had only happened once or twice before in my lifetime due to weather, but there it was.

Once again, without so much as a thought, we looked at each other, and Gary exited the bridge approach and hit the side streets of Fort Lee, and a few blocks away from the bridge entrance we parked the car. There was no other option, and I don't think either of us actually even considered going home, so we did what we had to do; we walked across the George Washington bridge with more than a foot of snow on the walkway, in suits and dress shoes, in below freezing temperatures with a wicked Hudson River wind blowing snow in our faces. We were to the best of my knowledge, the only people who walked across the bridge that morning.

We walked all the way across then several blocks to Washington Heights to the subway Station where I took the still operating "A" train downtown to my office, and Gary went off to his, arriving at our empty offices at around 9:30am. Even the people who lives in Manhattan and the five boroughs didn't dare come in that day; it was effectively a citywide snow day.

After about two hours of unanswered phone calls, I decided to call Gary at his office to see how he was doing, and the answer was the same; not a single office was open and not a single person was in.

We agreed that while our intentions were good, no matter how hard we tried that day the results would be zero. So, back we went, meeting at the subway and heading on the "A" train up to Washington Heights, walking back across the George Washington Bridge, and finally the very long and nerve wracking drive back "up" Skyline Drive, and home to Ringwood. Not surprisingly, Gary and I are still good friends today, 42 years later.

Am I bragging? Maybe a little, because as dumb and dangerous as it was, it is something that I am proud of having done. Am I suggesting you do this? No, but perhaps this story will help you to find your own internal barometer and determine how far you are willing to go and how bad you really want it, or as it was in mine and Gary's case, how bad you really NEED it.

EPILOGUE

In April of 2007, at the age of 74 I finally retired. From my first job working at my father's factory in 1948, until April 2007, I have worked every day for nearly sixty years, and I have done it through the following events:

- The birth of two children
- A near fatal bout of Blood Poisoning
- A near fatal bout with Hepatitis
- Two Open Heart Surgeries
- Three Angioplasty Surgeries
- The deaths of both of my parents
- My wife's two bouts with Cancer
- A lifetime of ups and downs

At 77, I honestly don't think I'm over the hill. I have just started on two new marketing ventures, and written this book, all of which will require all 42 years of my experience selling.

In the final analysis, isn't selling what it's all about anyway?

Good selling and good luck....but then again, there isn't any luck involved at all.

*As a final postscript, I wanted to mention (as I am sure that you noticed if you were paying attention) it was no accident or grammatical error that I capitalized the word 'Sales" more than 300 times in this book (314 to be exact); it is my way of finally giving "**Sales"** the respect it ultimately deserves...*

--Joe Sokoloff, *Salesman*

...J Tax Statement

Dept. of the Treasury • Internal Revenue Service

This information is being furnished to the Internal Revenue Service. If you are required to file a tax return, a negligence penalty or other sanction may be imposed on you if this income is taxable and you fail to report it.

These substitute W-2 Wage and Tax Statements are acceptable for filing with your Federal, State and Local Income Tax Returns. If you worked in multiple locations, or had several forms of special compensation, you may receive more than one of these documents.

All four copies of your W-2 are on this page, separated by perforations. The white copies are for your tax returns; the blue copy is for your records. General instructions for these forms, including an explanation of the letter codes used in box 12, are on the other side of the page.

To the right is an explanation of the contents of the wage boxes on your W-2. Please note that the Gross amount shown may include adjustments.

	Federal Box 1	Soc. Sec. Box 3 & 7	Medicare Box 5	State Box 16
Gross	600198.66	600155.66	600155.66	SEE
Deferred Comp.	18000.00			BOX 1
Group Term Life	2842.80	2842.80	2842.80	
Wages Over Limit		515098.48-		
W-2 Wages	586998.46	87900.00	602998.46	

2004

A. CONTROL NUMBER	2004 OMB NO.
B. EMPLOYER IDENTIFICATION NUMBER 23-2628762	EMPLOYEE'S SOCIAL SECURITY NUMBER
C. EMPLOYER'S NAME, ADDRESS, AND ZIP CODE ST IVES BURRUPS INC 1617 JFK BLVD STE 430 PHILADELPHIA PA 19103	13 Statutory Employee / Retirement Plan X / Third-Party Sick Pay
EMPLOYEE'S FIRST NAME AND INITIAL / LAST NAME JOSEPH H SOKOLOFF	14 OTHER NY DI 41.40

1 WAGES, TIPS, OTHER COMPENSATION	586998.46	2 FEDERAL INCOME TAX WITHHELD	188295.70
3 SOCIAL SECURITY WAGES	87900.00	4 SOCIAL SECURITY TAX WITHHELD	5449.80
5 MEDICARE WAGES AND TIPS	602998.46	6 MEDICARE TAX WITHHELD	8743.48
7 SOCIAL SECURITY TIPS		8 ALLOCATED TIPS	
9 ADVANCE EIC PAYMENT		10 DEPENDENT CARE BENEFITS	
11 NONQUALIFIED PLANS		12 a-d	C 2842.80 / D 18000.00

15 STATE	EMPLOYER'S STATE I.D. NO.	16 STATE WAGES, TIPS, ETC.	17 STATE INCOME TAX	18 LOCAL WAGES, TIPS, ETC.	19 LOCAL INCOME TAX	20 LOCALITY NAME
NY	232628762	586998.46	45392.64			

Copy C For EMPLOYEE'S RECORDS (See notice on back of copy B)

This information is being furnished to the Internal Revenue Service. If you are required to file a tax return, a negligence penalty or other sanction may be imposed on you if this income is taxable and you fail to report it.

These substitute W-2 Wage and Tax Statements are acceptable for filing with your Federal, State and Local Income Tax Returns. If you worked in multiple locations, or had several forms of special compensation, you may receive more than one of these documents.

All four copies of your W-2 are on this page, separated by perforations; the white copies are for your tax returns; the blue copy is for your records. General instructions for these forms, including an explanation of the letter codes used in box 12, are on the other side of the page.

To the right is an explanation of the contents of the wage boxes on your W-2. Please note that the Gross amount shown may include adjustments.

	Federal Box 1	Soc. Sec. Box 3 & 7	Medicare Box 5	State Box 16
Gross	723312.49	723812.49	723812.49	SEE
Deferred Comp.	18000.00			BOX 1
Other Pretax	700.00	700.00	700.00	
Wages Over Limit		633812.49-		
W-2 Wages	704812.49	90000.00	722812.49	

2005

A. CONTROL NUMBER	2005 OMB NO.
B. EMPLOYER IDENTIFICATION NUMBER 23-2628762	EMPLOYEE'S SOCIAL SECURITY NUMBER
C. EMPLOYER'S NAME, ADDRESS, AND ZIP CODE ST IVES FINANCIAL INC 1717 ARCH ST 31ST FLOOR PHILADELPHIA PA 19103	13 Statutory Employee / Retirement Plan X / Third-Party Sick Pay
EMPLOYEE'S FIRST NAME AND INITIAL / LAST NAME JOSEPH H SOKOLOFF	14 OTHER NY DI 52.20

1 WAGES, TIPS, OTHER COMPENSATION	704812.49	2 FEDERAL INCOME TAX WITHHELD	234613.05
3 SOCIAL SECURITY WAGES	90000.00	4 SOCIAL SECURITY TAX WITHHELD	5580.00
5 MEDICARE WAGES AND TIPS	722812.49	6 MEDICARE TAX WITHHELD	10480.78
7 SOCIAL SECURITY TIPS		8 ALLOCATED TIPS	
9 ADVANCE EIC PAYMENT		10 DEPENDENT CARE BENEFITS	
11 NONQUALIFIED PLANS		12 a-d	D 18000.00

15 STATE	EMPLOYER'S STATE I.D. NO.	16 STATE WAGES, TIPS, ETC.	17 STATE INCOME TAX	18 LOCAL WAGES, TIPS, ETC.	19 LOCAL INCOME TAX	20 LOCALITY NAME
NY	232628762	704812.49	54140.88			

2006

A. CONTROL NUMBER	2006 OMB NO.
B. EMPLOYER IDENTIFICATION NUMBER 23-2628762	EMPLOYEE'S SOCIAL SECURITY NUMBER
C. EMPLOYER'S NAME, ADDRESS, AND ZIP CODE ST IVES FINANCIAL INC 1717 ARCH ST 31ST FLOOR PHILADELPHIA PA 19103	13 Statutory Employee / Retirement Plan X / Third-Party Sick Pay
EMPLOYEE'S FIRST NAME AND INITIAL / LAST NAME JOSEPH H SOKOLOFF	12 OTHER NY DI 54.00

1 WAGES, TIPS, OTHER COMPENSATION	777268.48	2 FEDERAL INCOME TAX WITHHELD	251306.83
3 SOCIAL SECURITY WAGES	94200.00	4 SOCIAL SECURITY TAX WITHHELD	5840.40
5 MEDICARE WAGES AND TIPS	797268.48	6 MEDICARE TAX WITHHELD	11560.39
7 SOCIAL SECURITY TIPS		8 ALLOCATED TIPS	
9 ADVANCE EIC PAYMENT		10 DEPENDENT CARE BENEFITS	
11 NONQUALIFIED PLANS		12 a-d	D 20000.00

121